Reading, Writing, Playing, Learning

Finding the Sweet Spots in Kindergarten Literacy

LORI JAMISON ROG

DONNA-LYNN GALLOWAY

Pembroke Publishers Limited

Dedication

For all the teachers and children I have worked with over the years; my mom, dad, and husband Rob; and a special thanks to the Northern Lights networking group.

Donna-Lynn

For Jake, who will soon give some lucky Kindergarten teacher a run for her money and who is teaching me about love, language, and laughter all over again.

Lori

© 2017 Pembroke Publishers
538 Hood Road
Markham, Ontario, Canada L3R 3K9
www.pembrokepublishers.com

Distributed in the U.S. by Stenhouse Publishers
480 Congress Street
Portland, ME 04101
www.stenhouse.com

Funded by the Government of Canada
Financé par le gouvernement du Canada | Canadä

Ontario
Ontario Media Development Corporation
Société de développement de l'industrie des médias de l'Ontario

---

Library and Archives Canada Cataloguing in Publication

Rog, Lori Jamison, author
   Reading, writing, playing, learning : finding the sweet spots in kindergarten literacy / Lori Jamison Rog, Donna-Lynn Galloway.

Issued in print and electronic formats.
ISBN 978-1-55138-321-7 (softcover).--ISBN 978-1-55138-922-6 (PDF)

   1. Language arts (Early childhood). 2. Play. I. Galloway, Donna-Lynn, author II. Title.

LB1139.5.L35R65 2016   372.6'049   C2016-907634-2
                                        C2016-907635-0

Editor: Marg Anne Morrison
Cover Design: John Zehethofer
Typesetting: Jay Tee Graphics Ltd.

Printed and bound in Canada
9 8 7 6 5 4 3 2 1

FSC
www.fsc.org

MIX
Paper from
responsible sources
FSC® C004071

Acknowledgements

A special thanks to the following educators who shared their stories in this book:

- Nancy Carl, Grade 1 teacher and former Co-ordinator of Curriculum, Assessment and Instruction, K–5 Literacy and Early Learning, School District #43, Coquitlam, BC
- Lisa Commisso, Early Childhood Educator, St. Christopher Catholic Elementary School, Burlington, ON
- Katherine Dewar, Kindergarten teacher, Lumen Christi Catholic Elementary School, Milton, ON
- Kristy Doornbos K/1 teacher, McLeod Elementary School, Groundbirch, BC
- Jennifer Franklin, Grade 2 teacher, St. Mary Catholic Elementary School, Oakville, ON
- Ann George, Kindergarten teacher, Strawberry Vale Elementary School, Victoria, BC
- Shauna Lothrop, District Early Literacy Teacher, Quesnel, BC
- Lindsay McGregor, Grade 1 teacher, J.W. Gerth Elementary School, Kitchener, ON
- Christine Thomas, Data and Curriculum Co-ordinator, Elmira, NY

Some of the material in this book has been adapted from *Read, Write, Play, Learn: Literacy Instruction in Today's Kindergarten* by Lori Jamison Rog, International Reading Association, 2011.

Contents

Chapter 5: Shared and Guided Reading: The "We Do" of Reading Instruction   55

Chapter 6: Learning to Write and Writing to Learn   69

Chapter 7: Putting the "Play" Back in Word Play   77

Chapter 8: Celebrating Diversity in the Classroom   87

Introduction: Read, Write, Play, and Learn: Making the Case for Balance

First Day of School
Sheree Fitch

Here, take my child.
He has a fistful of crayons,
Is ready to begin
To enter the halls that smell of chalk dust and lemon oil.
He wants to colour a picture.
Help him to see that the colours he chooses,
The pictures he makes, are beautiful…
Before you ask him to paint the Sistine Chapel.
Here, take my child.
She knows one and one makes two.
I want her to learn to add,
Without being subtracted from.
I want her to multiply her abilities,
But not if it divides her against herself.
Here, take my child.
He has a book he wants to read.
Let him read it first,
Tell you why he likes it,
Before you ask him to read a book
You think he should read…
To be up to "the level".
Here, take my child.
She has written a poem:
"dandy lions are golden buttons in the grass"
Smell those dandelions, see the image,
Before you tell her dandelions are weeds or
Dandelions is not spelled correctly.
Here, take my child
but… TAKE CARE.

(Used with permission from the author)

If we could travel back in time to Germany in the mid-nineteenth century, we might be able to shake the hand of Friedrich Froebel, the man who "invented" Kindergarten. Froebel first conceived of early childhood education as a garden where children could learn and play. His "children's garden" focused on three areas of learning: toys such as building blocks for creative and constructive play; singing and dancing for healthy activity; and outdoor gardening for exploring the natural world.

Throughout much of the twentieth century, Kindergarten instruction in North America was influenced by the work of John Dewey, who believed that education based on co-operative behavior and sharing and caring for one another was what was needed to nurture the citizens of the future (Packett & Diffily, 2004). He urged that manual training, nature-study, and art be given precedence over the traditional "three Rs," and that there should be lots of opportunity for activities based on the children's interests. The dramatic play, construct-and-create, and discover-and-explore centres found in so many Kindergartens over the past few generations are the result of Dewey's influence.

For most of the history of Kindergarten, children were not expected to learn to read and write. From the 1930s to the 1960s, a philosophy based on "reading readiness" dominated Kindergarten instruction. Based on the principle that certain developmental markers had to be mastered before reading could take place, reading readiness advocates believed that it was not just unnecessary, but even damaging, to try to teach children to read before they were "ready." That magical moment of readiness was determined to be six-and-a-half years of age, based on the results of the 1931 reading tests in Winnetka, Illinois (Morphett & Washburne, 1931). Therefore, actual reading instruction didn't begin until the middle of first grade. Until that point, children were subjected to a range of exercises involving directionality, visual and auditory discrimination, and isolated letter work—anything but books.

In the mid-1960s, a reading revolution burst onto the scene. New Zealand researcher Marie Clay conducted an extensive study of the early reading behaviors of five-year-old Kindergarten students and concluded that young children could engage in letter and word identification, voice-print matching, and even self-monitoring. These were pretty radical ideas in an era when many people believed that reading instruction before the age of six-and-a-half was "futile if not deleterious" (Hiebert & Raphael, 1998, 5).

Perhaps, suggested Clay, the ability to make letter–sound connections is not the entry point into reading, but a medial step in a whole progression of behaviors leading to making meaning from print. In her 1967 doctoral dissertation, Marie Clay coined the term *emergent reading* to define the ongoing and developmental process of understanding and using written language from birth to independence.

This seminal research led to an increase in literacy activities in Kindergarten classrooms across North America. While read-alouds had always been an important part of the Kindergarten day, the shared-book approach (Holdaway, 1979) gave children the opportunity to view the print while listening to the story. Whole language advocates encouraged schools to immerse students in a print-rich environment and to integrate letter–sound instruction into experiences with connected print. Along with the housekeeping centres and puppet theatres and building blocks, teachers were encouraged to incorporate "literacy artifacts" such as books, notecards, and writing tools. Role-play reading and invented spelling were recognized as important steps on the journey to literacy. For the first time, kindergartners were expected to read and write as well as play.

Enter the National Reading Panel report of 2000 (NRP, 2000). This meta-analysis of the research on reading instruction concluded that systematic, synthetic phonics should be taught as early as possible. This study led to "No Child Left Behind," an important Act of Congress in the US, which increased academic demands on kindergartners and required educators to use specific "scientifically based" literacy programs. Recess, thematic learning, dramatic play centres, and discovery were replaced by didactic teaching and prescriptive programs. In many schools, you were more likely to see children sitting in desks completing worksheets than playing with blocks or playdough.

Play-Based Learning

Today, the pedagogical pendulum seems to be swinging once again. While many schools still maintain a highly academic approach, others are looking to Europe for models of play-based learning. The renowned project-based programs of Reggio Emilio, Italy, have had a profound influence on early childhood education throughout North America. In these schools, children are viewed as active constructors of their own learning, learning that is conducted through experiences with touching, moving, listening, and watching, as well as interactions with other children, their environments, and the adults in their world.

As ever, teachers are left struggling to find the balance. How much explicit instruction is appropriate—or necessary? Can children learn essential foundational skills through play? In this book, we are striving to support teachers as they seek the "sweet spots" at which learning through discovery is optimal or instructional intervention is necessary.

Kindergarten teachers have long found themselves caught in the tension between "child-centred" and "academically oriented" instruction. Play is the primary means by which young children make sense of their world and the social, physical, emotional, linguistic, and cognitive benefits of play are myriad. On the other hand, researchers like Judith Schickedanz (2004) caution that certain foundational literacy concepts such as letter names or initial consonants are often not "discoverable" and must be taught, especially to children who come to school with few literacy experiences. Obviously there is room for both in the Kindergarten curriculum. As Kagan and Lowenstein argue, "Diverse strategies that combine play and more structured efforts are effective accelerators of children's readiness for school and long term development" (2004, 72).

In fact, there is a wide spectrum between free play and didactic instruction. Kathy Hirsh-Pasek and her colleagues (Weisberg, Hirsh-Pasek, & Golinkoff, 2013) define a midpoint they call guided play, which involves creating structured environments to stimulate children's natural curiosity, discovery, and exploration while meeting specific curricular goals. Tools and tasks are carefully designed to allow students to explore and construct their own knowledge, with the support of sensitive questions and prompts from the teacher to guide the learning.

In her study of learning models in Kindergarten classrooms, Jennifer Russell (2011) observed that the majority of activities focused on academic goals but employed child-centred techniques such as constructivist learning and manipulating concrete materials. Even teacher-directed events often reflected playful overtones, such as games to reinforce letter–sound connections or high-frequency words. It all boils down to developmentally appropriate practice.

Developmentally Appropriate Practice

Kindergartners—and all children, for that matter—are best served by teaching that is appropriate to their developmental stage and sensitive to their individuality. At its foundation, developmentally appropriate practice is just good teaching. It is instruction that meets each child where he or she is on the learning continuum, then continuously scaffolds him or her to higher and higher levels of proficiency.

In 1986, the National Association for the Education of Young Children (NAEYC) released its first position statement on developmentally appropriate practice (DAP), in an effort to consolidate the rapidly emerging research on early literacy instruction. This position statement advocated a child-centred, play-oriented environment that offered children opportunities to explore literacy—if they chose to—with minimal teacher intervention. Some researchers determined that students in these types of environments were more motivated to learn and more confident about their own abilities (Stipek, Feiler, Daniels, & Milburn, 1995) and demonstrated higher achievement in later grades (Marcon, 2002). Others argued that the research behind developmentally appropriate practice was flawed and found no evidence that DAP improved either social or academic outcomes (Van Horn, Karlin, Ramey, Aldridge, & Snyder, 2005).

Prompted by a changing world of student demographics, increased expectations for student (and teacher) performance, and concern for children at risk of academic failure, the NAEYC issued a revised edition of its position statement on DAP in 2009. While maintaining its original belief in a constructivist, child-centred philosophy, the NAEYC also acknowledged the need for a balance of explicit instruction and modeling of critical skills.

In today's Kindergarten, it is generally agreed that children need more than just incidental experiences with print. The National Reading Panel (2000) advised that reading instruction should begin as early as possible, especially for vulnerable children who have not had rich experiences with print in the language of their school. The National Strategy for Early Literacy (Canadian Language and Literacy Network, 2009) asserts that most literacy challenges can be prevented through a mix of: a) effective instruction; b) early learning experience; c) systematic assessment to identify specific needs; and d) appropriate targeted intervention.

Dorothy Strickland (2008), a member of the National Early Literacy Panel (NELP), encourages a "peaceful coexistence" between developmentally appropriate practice and pressure to address the achievement gap that exists between our most vulnerable children and those that are more advantaged. She identifies three key characteristics of this balanced teaching:

1. It must be engaging and motivational, tapping into student interests;
2. It must be differentiated, stretching each child from where he or she is today to where he or she can be; and
3. It must involve explicit teaching with opportunities for guided practice in essential concepts and skills.

Whole class instruction should be brief, intentional, and multilevel.

Today's developmentally appropriate Kindergarten classroom is likely to include both direct instruction and unstructured play—and a myriad of activities in between. The classroom is full of print and other literacy artifacts that children are sometimes free to explore independently, sometimes invited to navigate with teacher guidance, and sometimes taught directly and explicitly. There are many opportunities for children to interact, plan, question, explain, problem-solve, and tell stories with one another and with the teacher. Children receive plenty of individual and small-group instruction targeted to their diverse needs and learning goals. There is a minimum of whole-class instruction; when it occurs, it is brief, intentional, and multilevel.

The NAEYC's 2009 position statement reminds us to think of developmentally appropriate practice not as "either/or" but as "both/and." Children must experience *both* explicit instruction *and* opportunities for free exploration and discovery. They benefit from *both* teacher-directed activities *and* spontaneous play. They thrive on *both* opportunities for choice and self-direction *and* clearly defined parameters for accepted behavior. They need *both* a positive image of themselves *and* a healthy respect for others who might be different from them.

Anne McGill-Franzen (2006) asserts, "If we are to improve literacy … we have to embrace the belief that teaching reading to five year olds can be a school experience that's every bit as playful, imaginative, inquiry-driven and developmentally appropriate as anything John Dewey or Jean Piaget might have dreamed up." (16)

When moving towards establishing a play-based Kindergarten classroom, I worried about how to address curriculum outcomes within an environment that allowed the students to explore and understand concepts and skills through play. I understood and valued the experiences that students could explore through play but was uncertain how the academic outcomes would be realized when the play was organized and initiated solely by the children. I came to realize that I, as the teacher, had an important role in developing and organizing opportunities for learning within my classroom. I needed to create playful experiences for students to engage in concept and skill practice. I moved away from independent practice with paper and pencil activities and toward a centre-based approach that allowed for interaction between students, materials, and skills/concepts. I carefully chose playful materials for the students to utilize at the centres so that student engagement and time on task was maximized (i.e., bean bags, bingo dobbers, giant die, smelly markers, magnetic wands, toy cars). What five-year-old would not want to throw a bean bag at a hopscotch grid taped to the floor to practice naming alphabet letters, practice letter sounds, or read the sight words they are learning? I began to think as a five-year-old and pay attention to what materials, formats, and experiences were appealing to them. There were plenty of ideas that at first seemed interesting and relevant but when put into practice were less than successful; however, these provided me with opportunities to reflect and refine my practice.

Shauna Lothrop, Kindergarten teacher

Reading and Writing All Day Long

We have long recognized the importance of filling children's world with print. That's why we teachers used to spend precious time and money creating elaborate bulletin boards, listing classroom "rules," and labeling everything in the room from the windows to the hamster cage. But too often that environmental print has lacked purpose, ignored by children at best and a distraction at worst.

The National Association for the Education of Young Children (2009) has cautioned against cluttering the classroom environment with purposeless print that tunes children out rather than engages them. Environmental print is just wallpaper unless it promotes student learning.

That's why today's Kindergarten is filled with environmental print that is created and usually initiated by the students themselves. Charts, signs, labels, directions, warnings, and instructions are just a few of the types of print that children create to send messages to others, record information, and document their own learning.

Walk into one of the classrooms in Donna-Lynn's district and you'll be surrounded by print. Not prefabricated bulletin board letters or careful teacher labels, but children's writing in all its many forms. A sign on the light table says, in invented spelling, "I mixed green and blue and it made turquoise." A sheet taped to a Straws and Connectors ™ construction says, "This is a mouse hotel." Paper ghosts swing from a clothes rack labeled "Haunted House." The attendance sign-in sheet next to the door features kid-written names reflecting various stages of development. This is a classroom in which writing reigns. A bulletin board displays an alphabet zoo. There are wonder walls and experience charts on which teachers record the students' ideas and questions. There's a traditional writing corner with postcards, different sizes of sheets of paper, and various writing utensils for children to write letters and messages and stories.

The children in Donna-Lynn's district know that writing is an important tool for giving instructions or sending messages to others. But it's also an important tool for documenting their learning, recording their thinking, and remembering their ideas. Long after the mouse hotel is disassembled and the haunted house is converted into something else, these students will have their drawings and/or writing to help them remember what they made, what they thought, and what they learned.

Environmental print also helps young learners see how important writing is in our world—all day, every day. Print tells us how to drive safely and when it's okay to cross the street; it tells us what's on television and where to find our favorite shows; it tells us how many scoops of sugar to put into our cookie batter and how to get to an unfamiliar place.

Thirty years ago, Jerome Harste (1984) and his colleagues reported that children as young as eighteen months old could identify the labels on familiar cereal, toothpaste, and fast-food packaging. These early experiences with the print in their world help children develop the understanding that abstract symbols can represent concrete ideas. At first, children recognize words as pictograms—the logo on the candy wrapper or the traffic sign—and don't make the connection to the individual letters S-T-O-P in a different context. But they start to develop the understanding that those squiggles called letters are put together in certain ways to make words and that the letters C-R-E-S-T say the same thing whether they're imprinted on a toothpaste tube or handwritten on a piece of paper. That's when familiar environmental print can be a useful tool in helping children print new words; recognizing, for example, *sting* has the same beginning sound as a known word *stop*.

Getting children to create their own print environment helps them use letters and sounds in meaningful, authentic ways. It reinforces that their voices are heard and that their ideas are important. It helps them learn and remember their ideas.

Not all Kindergarten children will be at the same stage of readiness to write at the same time. Drawing, scribbling, using invented spelling, and copying words from around the room must be accepted according to the child's stage of development. Only the teacher knows which children to nudge, which to support, and which to celebrate just where they are. But if we are to expect children to use reading and writing to learn, we need to provide them with opportunities for learning to read and write. That's where explicit instruction comes in.

The skills and attitudes that children acquire in Kindergarten will have a significant impact on their learning for years to come. In this book, we've attempted to provide a bridge between learning environments where children are free to interact with others, take risks, and make decisions about their own learning— and systematic instruction and practice in the skills and strategies of literate citizens. In the first section of the book, we share thoughts about what play and inquiry have to do with literacy, how the classroom environment, both indoors and outside, affects learning, and the importance of oral language development to all facets of learning. The second section of the book focuses on explicit literacy instruction: our children can't *read and write to learn* unless they have opportunities to *learn to read and write*. After much deliberation, we've decided to conclude the book with a chapter about celebrating diversity. It might be argued that addressing the needs of our most vulnerable children should have been the first chapter of the book rather than the last. However, research tells us that our at-risk learners need the same good instruction that the other students need, but they need it even more. That's why we chose to discuss best practices earlier in the book.

We recognize that this book is just a snapshot of effective practices in today's Kindergarten classrooms. There are many books that provide more detail on every one of the practices outlined here. (Lori has written some of them herself.) But, we trust that teachers will find some information that reinforces their own beliefs and practices, some ideas to supplement their Kindergarten programs, and, most importantly, some information that will lead them to further exploration, research, and experimentation.

We are delighted that several of our teacher–colleagues have been willing to share some of their stories and you'll find them throughout the pages of this book.

As the authors, we have experienced the same growing pains as many of our colleagues in the field. Both of us come from a traditional Kindergarten background. Lori was an early advocate of explicit literacy instruction in Kindergarten. Donna-Lynn was a leader in the full-day Kindergarten initiative in Ontario schools and is well-grounded in play-based learning. Most of the material in this book involved intense discussion, plenty of laughter, and lots of give-and-take as we struggled to find the "sweet spots" at which child-centered discovery and teacher-guided instruction co-ordinated most effectively. But, for both of us, it always boiled down to one thing: what's in the best interests of the children? That was always our guiding principle. And we learned to share our toys and play nicely in the sandbox. This book is the result.

1

Play-Based Learning in a Culture of Inquiry

Anyone who's ever been a kid knows what play is, right? Well, not necessarily. We can all recognize play when we see it, but explaining it is a lot trickier. Play is a complex set of behaviors that is actually quite difficult to define. It's generally accepted that an activity can be considered more or less playful, depending on the extent to which it is: pleasurable, intrinsically motivated, process-oriented, freely chosen, actively engaging the mind and/or body, and involving imagination or make-believe (Krasnor & Pepler, 1980; Rubin, Fein, & Vandenberg, 1983). In other words, running on the playground pretending to be superheroes and sitting on the floor sorting alphabet letters could both be considered "play," but would fall on different points on the "play spectrum."

Although purists maintain that true play exists without external motivation or adult intervention, there is increasing evidence that "guided play" can contribute significantly to learning (Weisberg et al., 2013). Guided play sits halfway between free play and direct instruction, with adult-scaffolded learning objectives incorporated into child-directed activity. "In guided play, teachers might enhance children's exploration and learning by commenting on their discoveries, co-playing along with the children, asking open-ended questions about what the children are finding or exploring the materials in ways that children might not have thought to do. Guided play always sees the child as an active collaborator in the process of learning, and not merely as a recipient of information" (105).

For example, sometimes children might be given an opportunity to play freely with a set of magnets. Or they might be invited to identify which objects are attracted by a magnet and which are not, and guided to construct generalizations about what makes an object magnetic. Although the latter example is extrinsically motivated and not freely chosen, it can still be fun, active, and engaging for children—playful learning, in other words. Most importantly, each activity is child-oriented—geared to the child's own interests and engagement. There is room for both types of play in today's Kindergarten classroom. In fact, one study which invited children to engage freely in object play before being asked to use those objects to solve a problem suggests that the previous examples with magnets might be even more effective if the children had an opportunity to play freely with the magnets before being asked to interact with them in a more directed way.

Although play is an important end in itself for children, it is also a means to other ends. Through play, children learn to co-operate and compromise, to lead and to follow. By pretending to be a parent or a baby, a firefighter or a teacher, children practice the norms of the culture in which they live. Play has been shown to have an impact on understanding the perspectives of others—an important foundation of empathy and social acceptance.

The physical, social, and emotional benefits of play are well-documented, but there are many cognitive benefits as well. Object and pretend play in particular have been linked to greater creativity and creative problem-solving (Russ & Wallace, 2014). The cognitive abilities that make up control of one's own thoughts, actions, and emotions, known as "executive function," are enhanced through play. These executive function abilities have been linked to the development of memory, attention span, and self-regulation, critical factors for success in school as well as in life. The famous Russian psychologist Lev Vygotsky believed that a child's greatest self-control occurs in play. But there are also many ways that play specifically supports the diverse knowledge and competencies we call "literacy."

Literacy and Play

There are three broad types of play, each of which contributes to language and literacy development in its own way. Pretend play entails creating alternate realities to the known world, with children either transforming objects into something else or enacting other roles themselves. Physical play involves the type of activities that the world associates most with the word "play"—running, jumping, chasing, climbing. And exploratory play invites children to discover and manipulate objects in their world using their minds and their senses.

Pretend Play is a foundational activity of early childhood. It can involve symbolic representation (transforming an object into something else, such as pretending a box is a spaceship) or socio-dramatic activity (in which the children themselves take on other roles). Vygotsky (1978) theorized that imaginative play develops symbolic, abstract thought, an important precursor to reading. For example, when children begin to use one object to represent another, such as pretending a block is a fire truck or a box is a rocket, they are developing the concept of symbolism, an important concept in a world of print, where ideas are symbolized by letters and words. Pretend play is also important to language development. During pretend play, children are found to talk more, speak in lengthier utterances, and use more complex language than when they are engaged in most other activities.

Pretend play also contributes to children's narrative abilities. They can understand and retell stories better when they've had opportunities to dramatize characters and events or settings. There's evidence to suggest that children's development of narrative skills is an important foundation of emergent literacy. Vivian Paley (2004) believes that in early childhood, "fantasy play is the glue that binds together all other pursuits, including the early teaching of reading and writing skills" (8).

There are many ways that teachers can provide opportunities and materials to support pretend play around literacy. Although many children will engage in make-believe regardless of the teacher's intervention, others might need a nudge in the form of costumes or puppets or modeling how to use these literacy artifacts. Some examples include the following:

- Create a classroom atmosphere that encourages and celebrates fantasy play.
- Create a "Kindergarten Costume Corner" with scarves, hats, glasses, and costumes for children to use for dress-up play.

- Gather puppets and stuffed animals related to books in the classroom library (fiction and nonfiction) for children to "read to" and to use for imaginative play about familiar stories.
- Provide a puppet theatre and puppets as well as materials for children to make their own puppets.
- Model the use of literacy artifacts as part of imaginary play.
- Invite children to "pretend you're the character" or act out a familiar story.
- Create one or more generic dramatic play centres that can be modified to meet the interests of the students, always ensuring that appropriate reading, writing, and drawing materials are available.
- Encourage imaginary play with constructions (e.g., blocks, Lego™, Knex™, etc.).

Physical Play is an important part of every child's development and may often incorporate pretend play and object play as well. When children chase one another, balance on a bench, climb a tree, kick a ball, or slide through a tunnel, they are engaging in the type of play that builds strength, endurance, co-ordination, and balance. But what does that have to do with literacy? Studies have shown that students who received additional physical activity time performed better on standardized assessments (Shephard, 1983) and that many students are likely to be more attentive in class after recess than before (Pellegrini & Davis, 1983). But more specifically, physical play builds the muscle strength and balance needed to be able to engage more productively in more sedentary learning activities. For example, do you have students who fidget during the read-aloud? It's possible that they simply do not have the core strength to maintain a sitting position for any length of time. As well, the ability to cross the centre-point in the body is an essential competency for both reading and writing, so it's important to engage in physical activities that require their hand or foot to move across the body and work on the other side, such as giving yourself a hug. Other examples of things educators can do include the following:

- Ensure that students have extended periods of time for indoor and outdoor gross motor play.
- Provide opportunities even within the classroom for physical outlets. For example, mark footprints for children to stand on to do wall pushups.
- Create conditions in the classroom that build balance and core strength, such as sitting on balance stools or exercise balls instead of chairs.
- Sing action songs and play games that require children to cross the centre point on their bodies, such as "windshield wipers" or "touch your left shoulder with your right hand." Have pairs of children sit back-to-back and pass a ball with both hands in a circular motion. Invite them to stand at a board (or outdoor wall) and make "crazy 8" shapes.
- Encourage weaving, drawing, and writing on large surfaces, such an outdoor fence or wall. Children can even "paint" the school wall with water.

Exploratory Play, sometimes called "object play," involves manipulating objects to create something new, to solve a problem or simply to learn more about them. Whether they're painting a masterpiece from watercolors, examining an owl pellet with a magnifying glass, or building a "mouse hotel" out of plastic straws, children are developing fine and gross motor skills. They are also strengthening such cognitive abilities as divergent thinking, problem-solving, and visual-spatial perception, while building schema about their world. One interesting study of block play (Hanline, Milton, and Phelps, 2010) found that preschoolers who had high levels of representation in their block constructions actually had higher reading abilities and a faster rate of growth in reading in early elementary school.

This type of "discovery play" is ubiquitous in Kindergarten classrooms, as we often display collections of interesting materials (such as water, sand, or even snow tables or collections of artifacts from nature) to stimulate children's interest and provoke further explorations. The famous psychologist Jean Piaget believed children were little scientists whose everyday "experiments" would reveal the nature of their world. Through solitary object play and exploratory play, children are introduced to the ways objects work ("What does it do?") and how they can exert control over those objects ("What can I do with it?") (Bjorklund & Gardiner, 2011, 154, 12). A child's first instinct, when presented with an unfamiliar object, is to engage in exploratory play, thereby learning not only more about the object itself, but building schema about that category of objects that they can transfer to others in a similar category. Here's where free and guided play can support one another: it's been shown that children who have opportunities to play freely with an object first are better at using that object to solve a problem assigned to them.

The Teacher's Role

Play time in Kindergarten is anything but free time for teachers. In reality, the teacher has a very complex job balancing a range of roles: onlooker, stage manager, co-player, and/or guide, depending on the situation.

The teacher's first task is to create a learning environment in which the children feel safe, comfortable, and free to take risks. Children need to be able to explore, experiment, discover, problem-solve, and interact with one another. The sensitive teacher knows when to provide support, when to ask questions and provoke thinking, and when to back away and leave the children on their own. It's an art that must be creatively sculpted so that the children can learn and grow as they play. Another important role of the teacher is to simply provide time. Experience tells us that children need a minimum of 30 minutes of uninterrupted time to plan, set up, and engage in higher levels of social and cognitive play.

At times, the teacher is watching, often documenting her observations and making plans for future teaching or appropriate interventions. This is a time to pause, watch, and listen. Taking pictures or making notes gives the teacher time to reflect on whether to intervene in the play and, if so, what language and actions will be appropriate to raise the level of the students' language and thinking.

At other times, the teacher may set the stage and manage activity by putting out new toys, materials, or objects to provoke thinking and encourage exploration. He will provide assistance when children need it, and might make suggestions for further exploration or discovery. He needs to seek out resources for children to research and record their learning. He might have to support the child who is lost or intervene in a situation where behavior is inappropriate.

The teacher can also be a co-player, playing along and negotiating the rules of the play on an equal footing with the other children, but at the same time, modeling social skills, language interactions, and problem-solving. At all times, however, the teacher's role is to ensure that all children are engaged, involved, and safe.

"Giving children the chance to freely experiment with diverse objects provides information about the world and the child's place in it, allows them to create and express themselves by making new objects or art, encourages creative problem solving, and builds the foundation upon which formal math and science training can be built." (White, 2012, 14)

Children need at least 30 minutes of uninterrupted time to fully benefit from their play.

The opportunities for exploratory play with objects are unlimited. Exploratory play is a wonderful medium for introducing new concepts, provoking further interest and research, and building our students' background knowledge about the world around them. There are many ways that educators can support exploratory play, including the following:

- Systematically introduce new toys, tools for creating and constructing, and objects for discovery.
- Provide opportunities for children to explore them freely before incorporating a problem or task.
- Invite children to provide items for discovery centres or collections of found objects.
- Encourage children to engage in group play to build language and social skills.
- Use careful teacher language to build vocabulary and invite higher-level thinking when engaging with children during their play. (See Chapter 3 for more information on teacher talk.)
- Create sensory exploration tubs with objects of different sizes, shapes, and textures. Make them available for free exploration as well as guided problem-solving. For example, the teacher might first allow the children to play with the objects, then invite them to sort the objects into categories, using rimmed cookie sheets divided into sections with masking tape.
- Engage children in conversation about their learning and encourage them to articulate their thinking or "name your learning."
- Ensure that there are always appropriate reading materials and writing implements to supplement the learning, to invite research, and to record ideas about their discoveries.

A Culture of Inquiry

As Curriculum Coordinator, Nancy Carl recalls the story of a teacher in her district who noticed that her students were particularly interested in water during their outdoor play. They were digging ditches and watching the flow of the water. Then they began building dams and rerouting the water. The teacher challenged the students with thought-provoking questions, such as: What do you think would happen if…? How could you…? What will you do next?

Capitalizing on her students' fascination with water, the teacher bought some PVC pipes and elbow joints and placed them in the water centre, where the students experimented with water traveling through the pipes. This led to questions about how water got into their homes, so the teacher arranged a field trip to the local water plant.

When the teacher tried to initiate a new project in the spring, the kids noticed the drains outside and they were off on the water challenges again.

By following the interests of the children, inviting their questions, supporting their research to find answers, and challenging their thinking, this teacher taught students that they were researchers and learners—in an inquiry that lasted almost all year long, with extensive learning across the curriculum.

Nancy Carl, Coquitlam, BC

When children engage in exploratory play, they are experimenting with the world around them. The Kindergarten teacher can turn these explorations into inquiries and investigations that lead to further knowledge and understanding of their world. These investigations require students to research, to count, to communicate, to document their ideas, and to work co-operatively together. These have always been important learning goals in Kindergarten. What makes today's Kindergarten different than in the past is the degree to which the interests of the students guide the direction of learning. Consider the "themes" of old, when we teachers selected a theme of the week or the month and constructed a set of activities to engage students in that theme. (How often did we add pictures of penguins or dinosaurs to math and phonics worksheets, just to comply with the given theme, even though they added nothing to the learning experience?) In today's inquiry-based learning, the teacher no longer has the heavy-duty front-loading and planning tasks; instead she now has the responsibility for carefully and sensitively guiding, supporting, and prompting students not only to self-regulate, plan, and implement their inquiries, but also to ensure that learning goals are addressed.

The citizens of today and tomorrow are faced with an explosion of information. It is guaranteed that we in school will never be able to teach students all the factual content in their world. What we do know is that we need to provide them with the skills they need to access that content, generally referred to as the "4 Cs of 21st Century Competencies": critical thinking, communication (written and oral), collaboration, and creativity (Government of Ontario, 2016).

Does it matter if our children leave Kindergarten without knowing the difference between a stegosaurus and an apatosaurus? Should we worry if they go into Grade 1 without knowing what a veterinarian does or what happens if the groundhog sees his shadow? What we want them to be able to do is access information from print, from technology, and from other people, and to communicate their learning in a variety of modes. We want them to know not just their number facts but how to use numeracy skills in the world around them. We want them to be able to co-operate with others, to ask and answer questions, to give and follow directions. In other words, we want them to be independent learners and curious, engaged citizens of the world.

Stages of Inquiry: Engagement

It was picture day at one of Donna-Lynn's schools and the kindergartners were particularly excited to be able to choose a background for their portraits. When they returned to the classroom, a large group wanted to set up their own photo shoot. The teacher watched and listened to their interactions with interest. What could she do to capture that excitement and extend their learning? She gathered the inquiry group together on the carpet and encouraged them to brainstorm about the equipment they would need: large paper, paint, a camera or tablet to take pictures, something to sit on. Soon, other children joined the conversation and, before long, almost the whole class was engaged in some aspect or other of this photo studio inquiry.

This is the "Engagement" stage of the inquiry process. The children wonder, question, and explore while the teacher serves as a facilitator, asking thoughtful questions to guide and focus the students' thinking. Questions that guide thinking include:

- Why do you think…?
- How might…?
- What would happen if…?
- What did you do…?
- What could you do…?
- What do you wonder…?

The challenge for the teacher is not to take over, but to be the "guide on the side." As much as possible, the children should be encouraged to direct their own discussion. As the children talk, the teacher records their ideas. This not only shows children what their "talk" looks like in "writing," it serves as an ongoing reminder of the ideas they generated.

When getting started with inquiry, bloggers Caroline Thornton and Shirley Silva (journeytogetherfdk.com) recommend: "Listen, listen, listen, not only with your ears but with your whole being." Often the children's curiosity and wonderings will be the inspiration to learning. Many classrooms have a "wondering wall" to inspire and record student questions. Some teachers cover the wondering wall with sparkly paper as a special invitation to ask questions. Many, but not necessarily all, of these queries will ultimately lead to further inquiry and research.

Sometimes teachers will offer a "provocation" to inspire student interest. Provocations, as the name implies, are intended to provoke thinking, questioning, discussing, and creating. In Kindergarten, a provocation is often an artifact, but it can also be a read-aloud or even a "big idea" question. The Kindergarten teacher who knows her students well is likely to have success inspiring the interests of her students. But if students aren't interested in a topic, abandon it. There will be many other avenues through which curriculum goals can be met.

Examples of Provocations

- An interesting book or picture
- Specimens from nature
- Concepts about how the world works (e.g., changing seasons, light)
- Familiar objects used in new ways
- An artifact such as a magnet or a map
- Unique materials for building or creating
- An important issue (e.g., bicycle safety or pollution)
- A special event or field trip

Stages of Inquiry: Investigation

The students decided they needed to create some scenic backgrounds like the ones the school photographer used. "How will you know what to paint on the background?" asked their teacher. The children decided that they needed to make some small sketches to see what designs they liked best and what details they would need to add. The day was done and the children put their plans on the "work in progress" shelf to clean up for the day. Would they have the same commitment to the project on the next day—or was it a fleeting moment of enthusiasm?

As she reflected on the day's experience, the teacher made a note to herself to revisit this experience later when the class talked about writing. The children made a plan and some rough sketches, and then went back and added details—in the same way that writers plan, draft, and revise their writing.

The next morning, excitement was higher than ever and the children could hardly wait to get into the classroom. They had come up with the idea that they needed props and costumes for the people to wear. Someone suggested they needed to make a brochure to let people know what choices they had.

During this time, their teacher was mostly on the sidelines, observing and documenting what the children were doing. She had to decide when to intervene, if at all, and what to say when she did. One of the students approached her with a problem: they needed some dedicated space and several pieces of furniture for their photo studio. A class meeting was convened and the students discussed whether it was all right for this group to use a corner of the room as well as a couch and chair in the classroom. The other students had no difficulty giving up the corner space; however, they weren't so sure about the furniture, as it was being used for other purposes. Ultimately, the class came up with a compromise that all could share. The teacher could have resolved the issue much more quickly with an arbitrary decision, but empowering the children to negotiate with one another built social and communication skills and brought ownership and co-operation to the process.

This is the "Investigation" phase of the inquiry process. Students become researchers as they try to seek answers to their questions by gathering, sorting, and interpreting information. They observe and evaluate their progress in their inquiry and make necessary changes.

Although we tend to think of research as combing through informational print or surfing the Internet, there are many other ways for kindergartners to gather information. Sometimes they will conduct hands-on experiments. At other times, they might look for an "expert" on the topic. Classes that are active in social media might ask their Twitter or Skype friends around the world for help. And, of course, there are print and online resources that will often require assistance from a teacher or another adult.

One little girl wanted to paint the "Paris tower" on a big canvas to use as a backdrop. With her teacher's help, she found a picture of the Eiffel Tower on the computer and set up her easel. Other friends joined in and together they painted a large mural of the Eiffel Tower. The students surveyed their classmates to see what backdrops others would like to choose and the beach was the clear winner. While some children painted a beach backdrop, others organized equipment for the studio: paint, paper, cameras, costumes, and props. They already had some experience with taking pictures using the classroom tablets, but they needed some practice with composing portraits of people and printing them on the color printer.

Stages of Inquiry: Communication and Celebration

Eventually, someone suggested that they might invite other classes to take advantage of their photo studio and the students created posters to distribute around the school. There was standing room only at the "official opening" of the photo studio. The photographers and their assistants helped monitor the crowd and pose the subjects with costumes and props. A mirror was set up for customers to check their appearances. One child was assigned the job of keeping records. Another had the job of saying, "1-2-3-POSE!" Finally, the photos were printed, placed in envelopes, and delivered to their "customers."

The final stage of the inquiry process is "Communication." A celebration of learning, such as the grand opening of the photo studio, is a terrific way to end an inquiry, but there should still be an opportunity for reflection, for sharing what was learned, and anticipating what might be done another time. At this point, the teacher's role is to help children distill what was learned from the inquiry and make connections between prior knowledge and new discoveries.

Habits of Mind

Inquiry has long been an integral part of such disciplines as science and technology. In the Kindergarten program, however, inquiry is not just a set of activities, but a "stance," a habit of mind that permeates all thinking and learning throughout the day. It is not limited to a subject area or topic, a project, or a particular time of day. It is not an occasional classroom event, nor an approach appropriate for only certain children. As noted in the curriculum policy documents in Ontario and British Columbia, inquiry is at the heart of learning in all subject areas. Educators use their professional knowledge and skills to co-construct learning with the children—that is, to support children's learning through play, using an inquiry approach.

> Rachel White (2012) of the Minnesota Children's Museum suggests that inquiry develops the following skills:
>
> *Pausing*: Give others time to think and complete their thoughts
> *Wondering*: Feel free to ask questions about things we wonder or don't understand
> *Focusing*: Stick to the topic or task at hand
> *Sharing*: Share our own ideas and piggyback on the ideas of others
> *Synthesizing*: It's okay to change our thinking as we learn new information
> *Proving*: Be prepared to explain our thinking and provide support for our ideas
> *Respecting*: Listen to and value the ideas of others, even if those ideas are different from our own

Inquiry places children's curiosity at the heart of learning. But just because children are empowered to ask, investigate, and answer their own questions, it doesn't mean that teachers are relinquishing their roles. It is the teacher's job to weave curriculum objectives and standards into the children's explorations. He asks careful questions to extend children's thinking. He provides resources and guides research. He invites children to use a variety of means to communicate their ideas with others. And he documents their learning, determining what each child knows and stretching each child to higher levels of literacy.

Not all children will follow the same paths. Different groups of students are likely to explore in different directions, even within the same inquiry, depending on their interests. Regardless of the direction of the inquiry, however, all children learn to ask questions and look for answers, interpret textual, visual, and oral information, record and reflect on their learning, communicate with others, represent their ideas, and co-operate to achieve a common goal. There are few educational routines that give us quite so much bang for our pedagogical buck.

I have always believed that play-based learning was the best approach to take when teaching young children and I embraced this as a Kindergarten teacher. After five years of teaching Kindergarten, I decided that I wanted to change grades and attempt to bring play-based learning into the higher primary years, so I began my journey teaching Grade 2.

In the beginning, it was not easy. I began the year doing what I knew best, setting out provocations with an intentional learning experience and allowing the children to explore. I believed that I was on the right track and felt confident that I was starting the year on the right foot. But then I began to doubt myself. I was new to the grade and watched all the other teachers teach in a very different way. I worried that I wasn't teaching my students everything that they need to learn. And yet, the children were engaged and taking responsibility for their own learning—and loving it. I was covering many subject areas and it was clear that play-based learning was working in my classroom.

As the year continued, our class exploded with inquiry projects. One of our read-alouds sparked the idea of starting a class store where the children would make items to sell to their friends in other classes. We brainstormed how this would fit into what we were learning in math, language, media, and drama. With guidance, the children began to plan their stores.

During this whole process, I had to keep the children focused on the learning. I outlined all the curriculum expectations that we would be covering and we co-created learning goals around them. Students worked in groups to create stores and advertisements. They recorded the hours that they worked and were paid for their time. The money they earned would be used to buy items at other stores in our classroom mall. This inquiry project made it very apparent that, even in Grade 2, play-based inquiry was a powerful structure for engaging students while "uncovering" the curriculum. In fact, some of my colleagues have decided to give it a try in their classrooms as well.

What an exciting learning journey for my students and me.

Jennifer Franklin, Grade 2 teacher

2

The Classroom Environment: The Third Teacher

In my first year of teaching Kindergarten, I was very concerned with the esthetics of the classroom. I wanted my classroom to look like a page from a magazine, with defined areas for play. When you walked into that room, I wanted you to know that over here we build stuff and in that corner, we draw and this table here is for practicing the words hanging above it. I spent so much time patrolling the classroom, saying, "Bring the markers to the table, please," "Don't mix those blocks together!" and "Puppets stay at the puppet theatre!" After two years, I changed schools and was placed in a classroom less than half the size of any previous room I had worked in. This brought on a whole new challenge for my vision of the perfect classroom. I struggled to arrange furniture, I had much less wall space, and I was forced to use different areas for more than one purpose. It was time to remove the limits I had placed on myself and my students. With my new outlook on the areas of activity in my classroom, students defined what they would do and where. Blocks became part of their dramatic play as they built rocket ships, concert stages, and aquariums. Writing opportunities followed the children around into all areas of the classroom, giving their writing tasks a purpose. Art activities were truly creations of their own, often making something to incorporate into play. This change made me realize the vision of the perfect classroom through the eyes of a child. By letting go of my magazine picture with the tidy classroom where everything had its place, we created a learning space that had few limits. As inquiries unfolded in our room, our classroom would transform. Virtually every space in the classroom would evolve to include our area of interest. This in turn propelled our questions and extended the interests and learning. My classroom at times can look like a form of organized chaos, but I know that there is rich and meaningful learning happening and that is not something you can see in a magazine.

Katherine Dewar, Kindergarten teacher

We know that children learn from their teachers and from one another. But we sometimes forget that there is also a third teacher: the classroom environment. Children interact and construct learning with the space around them, just as they do with the people within it. Theresa Gonsoski (2015) suggests that young children should be surrounded by a "yes" environment. The sad reality is that our youngsters probably hear the word "no" more than any other word! An affirming environment says "yes" to experimenting, risk-taking, questioning, and discovering. It is rich with materials that encourage exploring and creating. It says "okay" to making mistakes, causing messes, and sometimes even falling and getting up

Donna-Lynn even suggests storing writing materials in glass (gasp!) containers. Not only are they versatile and reusable, they present an opportunity to teach the children that some objects are more fragile than others and need special care, as well as to address what to do if a glass gets broken accidentally.

again. Although safety is always a primary consideration, we can't remove all risks. If they never fall, how will they learn to balance, to hold on, and to recover?

Ideally, the classroom environment is created collaboratively with the students. It should represent the values of the learning community, such as: a connection to families and cultures; opportunities for both active inquiry and quiet reflection; materials to stimulate curiosity and discovery; rich literacy artifacts to encourage reading, writing, and research; and structures to encourage interpersonal relationships. The right classroom environment enables us to meet students wherever they are developmentally.

The Indoor Classroom

It may very well be that the biggest challenge for today's Kindergarten teacher is giving himself permission to leave the walls bare. Rare is the Kindergarten teacher who doesn't spend the waning hours of summer vacation filling the classroom walls with posters, alphabet charts, labels, and signs—long before the children arrive. But recent research has shown that children may very well be more distracted than engaged by these environmental visuals (Fisher et al., 2014). These spaces that were once occupied by commercial and teacher-created materials are now *tabula rasa* waiting to display children's work and documentation of their learning. Soon these walls will be covered with anchor charts, experience charts, and children's drawings and writings—supporting not just literacy and learning, but also a sense of ownership and community in the classroom.

The second biggest challenge is reconsidering the teacher's desk. This large piece of furniture occupies a lot of prime real estate in the average classroom. Let's face it, how often do Kindergarten teachers get to sit down anyway? Is there another place for storing teacher paperwork and materials that would afford better use of classroom space? Or can the teacher's desk serve double-duty for children by attaching magnetic white boards to the sides or putting pillows for quiet time underneath?

In the past, we assumed that children were stimulated by bright, colourful surroundings. But now we recognize that pastels and soft white tones can have a more calming effect for some children. Low lights are more beneficial than fluorescents. Plants, soft seating, and even lamps make the classroom more welcoming and home-like. Classroom pets like a fighter fish, a hamster, or dwarf rabbit foster both caring and responsibility. You may also find it useful to have a message centre in the classroom. Many children take comfort in predictability and this can be a place to post labeled pictures of the schedule for each day.

Your Kindergarten classroom is likely to undergo many changes throughout the year to accommodate the varying needs and interests of the students. Donna-Lynn suggests considering the following when setting up the classroom at the start of the school year.

A space for large gatherings: Meeting space is needed for whole-class events, discussion, or instruction. This area should have enough room for all the students to sit comfortably and to see one another as well as the teacher. An interactive white board and gathering chair are often the focal points of this area.

Some teachers like to start the year by assigning each student to a spot on the carpet, but this shouldn't be a permanent situation; choosing a good spot to sit is an important part of self-regulation. Lori always has students sit with a partner during meeting times. She has created "partner sticks" by marking the bottom of craft sticks with different colors. Each student draws a partner stick and must pair up with the person who draws the same color. It's usually necessary to spend some time at the beginning of the year establishing routines for greeting and talking with partners.

Most Kindergarten classrooms have a carpet of some sort, but for those who don't, carpet samples from a local store can provide soft spots for seating. Hula hoops or even placemats can effectively delineate space for partner work.

Spaces for quiet thinking: Create nooks with soft seating and warm lighting for children to read books, work quietly with a partner, or simply contemplate life. A sofa or overstuffed chair invites children to take a break and decompress. Some creative teachers have even placed bathtubs or boats in their classrooms for children to curl up in.

Spaces for small group exploration and active play: These areas will take up most of the classroom space. A large space is important for gross motor movement. Consider placement of bookshelves, cabinets, and tables for ease of movement and teacher sightlines. Remember that not all children are sit-at-a-table learners; some learn best by lying on the floor, kneeling at low benches, or even standing up. Sitting on exercise balls or balance stools helps build the core strength that's necessary to sit for increasing periods of time. Keeping white boards, screens, and charts at children's eye level makes them more accessible to interactive learning. It's important that workspaces be flexible enough to be reconfigured for different situations and group sizes. It's better to be able to move furniture to accommodate larger groups than to limit group size. We want children to learn how to make room for others to join in.

Learning centres have long been a staple of the Kindergarten program, and they will vary according to space, resources, and beliefs of the teacher. Whether we call them centres or studios or simply materials storage, most Kindergartens will have some sort of space for a range of different writing tools, art supplies, construction materials, dress-up and drama artifacts, and books. Logistically speaking, placing the art studio near the sink and a mat under the sand table will make clean-up easier. Mount pictures of what the centre looks like when it's cleaned up; that will guide children in knowing where different materials belong. Although we have always advocated having a very special library corner or "book nook," we've also found that children are more likely to access reading materials that are strategically placed around the room, such as beside the classroom pet or the light table. And while we want our children to engage with fiction and non-fiction, there are many other types of literacy resources available. For example, you will want to include plenty of "functional" texts, such as store flyers, restaurant menus, and cookbooks. Ask parents to help you find reading materials in their children's first language, which may not be English.

Whether materials are defined as part of a "centre" or simply stored on accessible shelves, it's important that students have the freedom to mix and match and move them around. Many times, a project will require a range of items, such as craft items, found materials, books and paper, and perhaps some building blocks.

In terms of storage, let's not forget accommodating some space for storing the children's personal materials. Most classrooms have some sort of space for outdoor gear, whether it is cubbies or just hooks on the wall. Magazine holders (cardboard or plastic) can be used as individual book boxes. Another set of magazine

"Traditional centres have become places of discovery and wonder in my play-based classroom. Objects that might interest a child, entice them to ask questions and want to learn more, spark wonderings, and provoke learning are placed in intentional areas around the classroom. Within these centres, children share their previous knowledge, ideas, and wonderings. Educators then support that interest by highlighting the child's knowledge, their language, and asking more questions to challenge their thinking and promote conversation."

Lisa Commisso, Early Childhood Educator

holders (or large cereal boxes, peanut free, of course) may be used for children to store individual projects in progress. For projects too large to store in boxes, bright orange toy pylons can be used to protect projects under construction.

It's not necessary to make all supplies available right from the start. In fact, it's wise to start with just a minimal amount of materials so children can practice using and caring for them. That way, it's an exciting event each time new tools, artifacts, and creating/constructing materials are introduced throughout the year.

A discussion of the classroom environment would not be complete without mentioning the other adults in the classroom—volunteers. Volunteers play a key role in supporting the classroom program. They can read and sing to the children in English or in their first languages—and listen to children read themselves. They can engage with the children in their independent or guided play. Volunteers can enrich the classroom experience with a range of talents, such as knitting, drawing, doing yoga, or playing a musical instrument.

Our children's learning is significantly impacted by the physical and social space in which they exist. But that isn't limited to the indoor environment. In fact, there's increasing evidence that children should be spending a lot more time outdoors—in school and at home.

The Outdoor Classroom

In many parts of Europe, outdoor play is an essential part of every child's day.

Enter this Kindergarten classroom in one of Donna-Lynn's schools and you might see a group of children bent over an anthill watching a trail of ants moving back and forth. Another group is kicking a soccer ball across a grassy knoll. Some are riding tricycles across the tarmac and some are sitting at a picnic table in the sun, building with blocks or writing stories. If this doesn't look like your typical Kindergarten classroom, there's a good reason. That's because it's outside.

More and more schools are acknowledging the importance of outdoor play as part of the curriculum. There's a major concern in North America that our kids are not getting enough exercise; however, much of the research on outdoor learning as an extension of the indoor classroom is coming from the United Kingdom, where outdoor play has been identified as an essential part of early childhood education, and Scandinavia, where *udeskole* is part of every child's day. In fact, a report from the Norwegian government over 50 years ago recommended that students spend not more than *two hours a day indoors*!

The Early Years Foundation Stage framework, which sets the stage for birth to age five learning in Great Britain, states that "being outdoors has a positive impact on children's sense of well-being and helps all aspects of children's development." We know that exercise, fresh air, and sunshine contribute to physical health. As well, outdoor play seems to support emotional development, as children are more likely to move away from confrontation and less likely to demonstrate frustration than when they are indoors (Ouvry, 2003). And it promotes pretend play, especially for boys, who often fantasize about superheroes that run, chase, and fly.

Certainly, spending part of the school day outdoors is nothing new in our schools. But the traditional recess, while welcomed by children for its social and physical benefits, has never been particularly valued as a curriculum enhancement by the educational establishment.

In most of our schools, learning outside the classroom has tended to be a special event rather than an integral part of the school day. The "field trip" has been a ubiquitous aspect of every child's school experience, whether that "field" is a museum or a marsh. But, outdoor learning need not involve traveling on a school bus or even trekking down the street. Supporters of the "outdoor classroom" advocate making the school grounds an extension of the indoor classroom, allowing students to move in and out fluidly as they desire.

That's a scary thought for many of us in North American schools. What about supervision? What about equipment? What about appropriate clothes and footwear? In fact, three of the biggest arguments against outdoor classrooms involve cost, weather, and safety.

Of course, the children's safety and security are always important considerations, but, to quote Play England's 2013 position statement: "We must not lose sight of the important developmental role of play for children in the pursuit of the unachievable goal of absolute safety" (np).

In truth, the research suggests that safety is not as big an issue as we may think. A major international study conducted by David Ball of Middlesex University in England reported that the risk factors of playground play are minimal, particularly when factored against the benefits. Ball (2002) reported that the most common injuries are from falls, a risk that can be further minimized by ensuring that no play structure is higher than 1.5 metres (5 feet) tall. Psychologist Peter Gray (2014) has written extensively about the importance of "risky play," stating that injuries are far more likely to happen in organized sports than in free play. Secure entrances, exits, and boundaries are essential so that children can explore freely in the outdoors, but they should be encouraged to make appropriate choices and given opportunities to manage risk themselves.

Cost is another concern when establishing an outdoor curriculum. But an outdoor classroom does not require elaborate and costly equipment. In fact, some research has shown that children would rather have materials that they can move and manipulate themselves than fancy play structures. Ask parents and caregivers to be on the lookout for free and inexpensive materials that might enhance the outdoor classroom. At one school, a parent who was a firefighter managed to scrounge some oversize fire truck tires that served a variety of uses in the outdoor school. At another school, some parents discovered that the municipality was giving away free compost. The adults picked up the compost, brought it to the school, and helped the children unload, dump, and spread it on the children's garden.

Planning an Outdoor Classroom

Elements to consider when planning an outdoor classroom environment include spaces for nature study, for quiet contemplation, for active play, for creative endeavors, and for group gatherings.

Natural Spaces. "Wilderness" areas such as fields and woods are often more appealing to children than adult-created and -managed play spaces. Research from Scandinavia reports that children who play in natural landscapes demonstrate better motor fitness, balance, and co-ordination, as well as more creativity in their play—than children who played in a traditional playground (Fjortoft, 2001).

Learning outdoors also helps children understand and appreciate the way nature is constantly changing with the weather and throughout the seasons. Even a small corner of the playground can make for fascinating study. For example,

Oversize tires from tractors, semis, or firetrucks can serve many purposes, such as seating space and climbers. Smaller tires may be filled with dirt to create self-contained gardens. (For safety, just make sure the steel bands on the side are not sticking out.)

Allow the children to paint the tires! Not only does this make the space more colorful and attractive, it also helps to build a sense of ownership.

Perhaps you can negotiate with your custodian a "no-mow" zone on the school lawn for long grass to grow. The children can observe, draw, and write about the different creatures that they notice in the grass.

the Square of Life project (http://www.k12science.org/curriculum/squareproj/) invites students to mark off a square metre of their playground space and observe it for changes in living and nonliving things over the course of time.

Growing Spaces. Froebel was the first to recommend that every early childhood setting have a place for children to grow plants; hence the origin of the term *kinder garden.* Raised beds, empty tires, pots, and hanging baskets can all provide opportunities for digging, watering, weeding, and nurturing plants, from herbs and vegetables to flowers and shrubs. Hardy plants, such as sunflowers, pumpkins, tomatoes, and zucchini, may be planted in the spring and will be ready to harvest when the students return in the fall.

Active Spaces. An important part of outdoor play is gross motor movement. Much outdoor activity requires no special equipment—just space to run, jump, skip, and chase. However, if finances permit, low climbers, balance beams, ladders, tunnels, nets, and rope swings might be installed. Teach children about managing risks and expect them to take responsibility for their own safety. And let's not forget about wheeled toys such as wagons and tricycles. (Check on the rules in your community; in the province of Ontario, for example, it is not required that children wear helmets while riding in school playgrounds but it is necessary on sidewalks and in public areas.) Provide children with tools for creative, large movement play, such as beanbags, hula hoops, parachutes, balls, and bats. Climbers should not be higher than 1.5 metres or 5 feet. And things to climb *over* and *into,* like big logs, are often more engaging than things that are high.

Quiet Spaces. Are there calm places in your outdoor environment for quiet contemplation or reflection? Ideally, these are created from nature, such as a space enclosed by bushes, but may also include a play house or other constructed space. Add rugs, cushions, or seating. One of Donna-Lynn's schools took advantage of a tree that had fallen in an ice storm and they had the trunk cut into logs for seating.

Creative Spaces. Creating sculptures and collages from found materials are logical activities for outdoor spaces, but writing, drawing, completing puzzles, and playing with blocks can also go on outdoors. Child-size picnic tables facilitate some of these fine-motor activities. As well, take advantage of the unique offerings of the outdoor space: chimes and other sound-making tools; chalk drawing or painting on concrete or asphalt; explorations of light and shadows. The chain-link fences that surround most schoolyards offer unlimited possibilities for weaving, hanging creations, and holding boards for writing, painting, and sending messages.

Gathering Spaces. Are there spaces for large or small groups to gather for discussion and instruction? Knowledge circles or other large group gatherings might entail some explicit instruction, a read-aloud or shared reading experience, or a group discussion. Sometimes a group meeting is needed to solve a problem. For example, one of Donna-Lynn's classes got so excited about digging holes all over the garden that safety became a concern. The children held a meeting and decided that there should be an area of the playground designated for digging. They chose one spot where anyone could dig and look for worms, potato bugs, or centipedes without causing danger to others, and marked it with a sign that said "Dig Zone."

Of course, the outdoor classroom will change and evolve according to the interests and curiosity of the students, just as with the indoor classroom. If you're just getting started with outdoor learning, invite the children to help create the space. They can draw plans and brainstorm solutions to any challenges. This will generate excitement and create ownership in the space.

There are many ways that the curriculum might be brought outdoors. Rather than boarding a bus to visit a fire hall during Fire Safety Week, invite a firefighter to visit the school. Children can explore the fire truck and other equipment up close and practice safety measures such as "stop, drop, and roll" on the school grass. In one school, a little boy's fascination with forklifts led to a surprise visit from a forklift driver, and he even got to ride on the forklift and press the button to raise the fork. Of course, the student had to write a letter to ask about the forklift and then to thank the driver for bringing the forklift to school. What a powerful use of authentic print!

The outdoor environment also lends itself to content learning—and not just in science. Counting seeds, adding and subtracting piles of leaves, measuring water from a fountain, sorting shapes, and even tracing letters in the dirt all bring core learning to life, and are much more meaningful than counting plastic bears or sorting buttons in the classroom. Clipboards can make documenting learning more portable and "grown-up" for kids.

Opportunities to engage children with the natural world reinforce Aboriginal teachings.

The outdoor classroom is an excellent place to reinforce Aboriginal perspectives. Although First Peoples across North America are very diverse, they have in common a respect for and connectedness with the land. Remember that these are the traditional custodians of the lands on which most North American schools are located. Opportunities to get students engaged with the environment align with Aboriginal perspectives. Add elements of storytelling and visits from elders and other leaders to help children explore and understand their relationship with the natural world. In Toronto's public schools, each day begins with an acknowledgement that the schools are situated upon traditional territories and a recognition of the enduring presence of Aboriginal peoples on the land.

Literacy and the Outdoor School

The outdoor environment affords many opportunities to build new vocabulary and concepts.

Obviously, outdoor environments lead naturally to explorations in science and math. But what about literacy? The same oral language benefits that result from indoor play also apply to outdoor play. Children have more opportunities to talk to one another, to ask and answer questions, to give and follow directions, negotiate, brainstorm, and to solve problems. The outdoor environment is an ideal place to build new vocabulary; for example, scientific terms such as names of plants or weather words, as well as attribute words relating to size, shape, color, and texture. Positional language—*behind, in front of, beside, on top of, underneath*—can be surprisingly challenging, especially for English language learners, but can frequently be reinforced in the outdoor classroom. Children also learn to hear and use comparisons: "that leaf is as big as my hand." Then there are the traditional childhood games—skipping songs, clapping rhymes—that build vocabulary and fluency with rhythm and rhyme. As well, all the guidelines for "teacher talk" in the indoor classroom (see Chapter 3) also apply here, though it's usually easier for most of us to engage in this dialogue during quiet activities than while trying to skip alongside a five-year-old.

The outdoor environment is an ideal place to "make marks," with chalk on brick or asphalt, with paint on stones or sticks, with marker or crayon on paper. At the start of the year, many of our kindergartners will be just beginning to explore letters and sounds. They might look for alphabet letters in the environment. Children can also be encouraged to trace letters in sand or dirt, or to form their names and other words with natural objects. Some teachers have painted alphabet letters on smooth stones (though children might be encouraged to do this themselves) or pieces of wood, offering more provocations for children to explore the alphabet in nature.

Using writing and/or pictures to document learning is as important in the outdoor school as it is in the indoor classroom. Recording observations of changes in the environment, making signs for the playhouse, or writing a reminder that more black markers are needed in the writing pail are all ways that children authentically use writing in the outdoor classroom. Clipboards are essential tools for writing "on the move" and make youngsters feel very grown-up. Child-size picnic tables make sit-down activities a little more comfortable. Basically, the same collections of books, paper, and writing utensils should be accessible in the outdoor classroom as well as in the indoor.

Explorations in the outdoor environment inevitably lead to more questions; books, magazines, and tablets (with protective covers) are important sources of research. The teacher helps the children access the information they need in order to answer their questions and to provoke further inquiries. But sometimes it's nice just to be able to read recreationally outside. One school had a plastic pool full of books where children could sit and browse in the "reading pool."

Ultimately, we can all become comfortable with the idea that the same instructional opportunities are available in the outdoor classroom as indoors.

Other Considerations for the Outdoor Classroom

Access to water: Water is a must for outdoor spaces, from fountains for drinking to fountains for aesthetics, pails for pouring and watering plants, and for cleaning up. Water may be used for music, art, and scientific explorations. Your relationship with your school custodian just may make the difference between hauling pails and getting a hose connection in your outdoor classroom!

Appropriate clothing and footwear: The weather shouldn't be the determining factor in whether children play and learn outdoors. There are few things more tempting to a five-year-old than a fresh mud puddle! Be sure to communicate the importance of having boots and waterproof outerwear (plus warm hats and mitts) readily available, and a spare set of dry clothes on hand. Inexpensive plastic ponchos may be purchased and kept on hand at school as well.

Tires: Tires of all sizes can be a real bonus for the outdoor classroom. Oversize tires from tractors or trucks can be used for everything from quiet gathering spaces to raucous climbing structures. Smaller tires can be filled with dirt to create self-contained gardens.

Fences: Most school playgrounds are surrounded by unattractive wire fences. Children can turn these fences into works of art by tying on or weaving strips of colorful plastic through the wire mesh. Or turn the fences into musical instruments by attaching pots, pans, metal lids, serving spoons, and other objects that can be used to make noise. Slice pool noodles in half and attach them to the fence at different levels for children to experiment with rolling marbles and other small objects or pouring water. A board on the fence can be used as a paint easel, a place to write or paint.

Portable supply cart: Scrounge old wagons for storing pots of paint, markers, chalk, crayons, and other mark-making supplies. Not only will this make the supply kits mobile, it will also encourage children to clean up after themselves.

Time: The traditional 15- to 20-minute recess is simply not enough time for outdoor learning. In fact, teachers who have implemented outdoor classrooms have found that children, especially boys, tended to choose big-movement activities such as running, chasing, or kicking a ball first. It seemed that most of them needed a good 30 minutes or more for physical activity, then they naturally drifted to more small-muscle movement activities, such as reading, drawing, writing, building, or gardening.

The Role of the Adults

> **"What's important is that children have an opportunity to bond with the natural world, to learn to love it and feel comfortable in it, before being asked to heal its wounds.... If we want children to flourish, to become truly empowered, let us allow them to love the earth before we ask them to save it."**
>
> David Sobel (1996), *Beyond Ecophobia*

In her study comparing indoor and outdoor classrooms, Ann Barbour (1996) found surprising differences in the roles and behaviors of the adults involved. One unexpected finding was that the outside was the environment of relative change and the inside was the environment of relative stability. For example, the indoor class tended to have more controls and restrictions, as if the walls and doors were metaphors for the kinds of teaching and learning taking place. This was not necessarily negative. Predictability can enhance a feeling of security for children; as well, there were closer physical contacts between children and adults within this secure enclosure. On the other hand, the outdoor environment had fewer restrictions and more unpredictability. There was less adult intervention in children's play, other than joining in the play alongside the children.

Also interesting was that there was less need for behavior management in the outdoor environment. Behaviors that are discouraged in the indoor space, such as loud voices, running, and throwing, are accepted and even encouraged outside. Educators reported that children were better at self-regulating and solving their own problems. The children rarely asked to go inside, even when the weather was cold or wet. And incidents of cuts requiring bandages decreased substantially!

In the outdoor environment, the educator has three main roles: interacting with children, ensuring their safety, and planning for future instruction. Of course, as with any aspect of the school day, communicating with caregivers is another high priority for teachers. Regular positive communication brings parents on board with a learning situation that may be unfamiliar to them and invites them to be part of creating and recreating the outdoor classroom.

Ask any kindergartners where they prefer to play and they're likely to answer, "Outside." The outdoor classroom provides opportunities to foster children's learning using the natural environment, and to gain knowledge and skills that promote interactive engagement, imagination, and self-regulation that supports balanced learning in the Kindergarten program.

3

Floating on a Sea of Talk: Oral Language Development

Linguist James Britton famously said, "Talk is the sea upon which all else floats." Why is oral language so important to literacy? Knowing how words go together in talk provides important syntactic cueing systems for reading and writing. Weak oral language skills can have a long-term impact on children's literacy development. Leah McGee and Donald Richgels (2003) reported that children with delayed spoken-language development are far more likely to experience reading difficulties than children with well-developed spoken-language abilities.

It seems these days that more and more children are arriving in Kindergarten without strong oral language skills in the language of instruction. Even children for whom English is their first language are experiencing more articulation issues and more trouble communicating their ideas. Most telling, they have smaller vocabularies, especially students in low socio-economic communities. Research confirms these observations. In Betty Hart and Todd Risley's (1995) classic study, they reported that preschool children from affluent families are exposed to about 30 million more words than children of poverty. In other words, even before these children show up at our classroom doors, there is already an exponential difference in their experience with words! When Lori's three-year-old grandson says, "Actually, Grandma, it's complicated . . .," she can't help but compare his language to the six-year-old who came to her with a skinned elbow crying, "Teacher, I hurt my arm knee."

We already know a lot about supporting oral language development in the early childhood classroom. Although articulation difficulties are generally the domain of speech-language experts, issues with communication, phonological awareness, and vocabulary are usually the responsibility of the classroom teacher. Unfortunately, many Kindergarten classrooms focus too much on print-related activities and too little on speech-related activities. We owe it to our children to provide a balance of both.

Communication

Different cultures have different language conventions, and simple gestures or tones of voice may be interpreted in diverse ways.

Many young children are unaware that the language we use varies, depending on the circumstances, audience, and purposes for which it is intended. We speak differently when we are talking to a baby than when we are presenting a paper at a university or delivering a toast at a wedding. This is the *function* of language, also known as *pragmatics*. As adults, we are accustomed to changes in language, style, tone, and even body language, such as gestures, eye contact, or the distance one speaker stands from another. But these subtleties are often not evident to children.

Students in Kindergarten must learn that spoken communication changes in different situations. For example, we use different voices, and even different words, on the playground than we do in the classroom. When children understand the pragmatics of oral language, they are better able to understand that "book language" is usually different from conversational language. Like oral language, the vocabulary, style, and structure of book language will differ for different types of texts.

Another important aspect of oral language is form, or *syntax,* which refers to the conventions that govern how words go together in our language. Formal grammar, parts of speech, and sentence structure are aspects of syntax. Oral language syntax is an important cueing system for solving difficult words; knowing how words fit into phrases or sentences can guide readers in anticipating what word might come next and confirming whether that word makes sense in the passage. By the time they reach Kindergarten, most children are able to use standard language forms most of the time, although some irregular forms may appear, such as "I brang it" or "I goed there." Consistent modeling and many opportunities for talk in the classroom will help all children develop those critical oral language foundations for spoken and written communication.

Syntax **refers to the conventions that govern how words go together in our language, and includes grammar and sentence structure.**

Teacher Talk to Support Oral Language Development

Children develop oral language skills by hearing and practicing talk. Unfortunately, much classroom talk focuses on basic procedures or management issues; even when discussing ideas and asking questions, teachers often tend to solicit brief responses from students and offer just a few words of feedback. The richest dialogue among teachers and students usually occurs during independent exploration and play times. Here are some guidelines for ways that teachers can support oral language development as they circulate among the students:

- **Pause before plunging in**: Take a minute to watch the children before becoming involved in the conversation. Think "OWL": Observe, Wait, Listen. This moment of hesitation affords time for the teacher to reflect on what to say—or whether to intervene at all.
- **Be conversational more than interrogational**: As teachers, our first inclination is often to ask a string of questions. There's nothing wrong with questions, as long as they don't turn into an interrogation. Ask authentic questions as part of a natural conversation. Here's a hint: don't ask questions for which you already know the answers!
- **Model and demonstrate language patterns**: Take advantage of opportunities to model grammatically correct language without judgment; for example, if a child says, "I brang it to school," you might respond with, "When you brought it to school, what did you do with it?"
- **Use rich vocabulary**: Getting involved in children's play enables us to introduce interesting and unfamiliar words. We can participate in the conversation and restate what children have said, using richer vocabulary, such as, "What equipment do you need to construct the rest of the snail playground?"
- **Repeat Vocabulary**: Children need multiple exposures to a word in difference contexts before they can make it their own. Visual, auditory, and even kinesthetic cues can help reinforce new vocabulary.

- **Extend and prompt**: Invite children to elaborate on their narratives. Don't accept one-word answers; prompt them to tell more, add more details, or give proof.
- **Don't forget wait time**: When we teachers ask a question, we tend to wait only one or two seconds before moving on to someone else or giving the answer ourselves! Some of our students, especially boys, have not even processed the question in that time. The research on wait time is powerful. Allowing three seconds of "think-time" seems to be optimal for raising students' thinking and responses. The same applies to wait time *after* a student answers a question! During the pause, students are quite likely to extend their thinking, add more information and elaborate on their responses.
- **Strive for five**: Extended conversations are more effective than one-shot question and answers. David Dickinson (2001) suggests that an effective conversation should go back and forth at least five times.

Language Games

In addition to incidental conversations between teachers and students during play and exploration times, there are many ways to support language development more deliberately through games and playful activities:

- *Question and answer games* such as "Twenty Questions" require students to ask and answer "yes" or "no" questions in order to guess a person, place, or thing.
- *Daily "newstelling" routines* help students communicate ideas and learn about the world.
- *Narrative activities* such as retelling and role-playing stories may go on informally in the reading corner or a dramatic play centre, or they might be introduced intentionally by the teacher. One way to formalize this activity is to create sets of cards with characters (a little girl, a scary monster, a new puppy), settings (the playground, the moon, on the school bus), and situations (getting lost, receiving a present, playing with a friend). Students draw one of each card and work in pairs to create a story around them.
- *Descriptive games* like "I Spy with My Little Eye" teach students to identify attributes of objects, such as size, shape, texture, or color. Extend the descriptions by adding sensory details and similes, like "it smells like" or "it's as round as…."
- *Barrier games* have two students sitting on either side of a barrier that prevents each of them from seeing what the other is doing, like the game of Battleship. (The barrier can be as simple as a book propped up between them.) Both students have the same set of materials. One student describes a design for the other student to re-create. This might be a pattern block design, a simple drawing, or duplicate sets of removable stickers on a background. It requires the describer to use very specific procedural language (including prepositions and attributes such as size or color) and the listener to follow directions. Both children need the same objects; start simple and get more detailed.

Phonological Awareness: Hearing the Sounds in Words

What's a word that rhymes with "ball"? What word do you get when you blend the sounds /m/-/o/-/p/ together? What sound is left when you take the /p/ off "pink"? What word do you get when you replace the /st/ in "star" with /f/?

It's likely you had no problem answering any of these questions. If you were a kindergartner, we'd feel pretty confident that you either know how to read or will learn to read with ease. Many studies have shown that this ability to hear, distinguish, and replicate the sounds in words—known as *phonological awareness*—is significantly correlated with learning to read.

Often the term *phonological awareness* is used interchangeably with the more specific term *phonemic awareness*. However, phonemic awareness refers to an understanding of *phonemes*—the smallest units that make up the speech stream (such as the sound of /p/ or /ch/) while phonological awareness is a broader term that includes larger sound chunks, such as rhymes and syllables.

TABLE 1 DEVELOPMENT OF PHONOLOGICAL AWARENESS SKILLS

Phonological Awareness Skill	Sample Task	Relationship to Reading
Recognition of Syllables	Clap as you say each part of the word: *play-ing*. How many parts do you hear in *holiday*?	The ability to hear large "chunks" of sound generally develops well before reading, but supports later reading of rimes or word families.
Identification of Individual Sounds	Which words start the same: *car, cat, lock*? Which word doesn't belong: *pin, tip, fin*?	The ability to focus on which elements of sound make words sound the same or different is an important precursor to reading.
Phoneme Blending and Segmenting	What word do you get when you blend together /m/.../a/.../p/? How many sounds do you hear in *sit*?	The abilities to blend and segment the sounds in words are likely to develop along with reading ability; each supports the development of the other.
Syllable Splitting and Phoneme Manipulation	What sound do you get when you take the /l/ off *land*? What word do you get when you change the /a/ in *pat* to /o/?	These advanced skills probably develop as a result of learning to read, as they are difficult without well-developed spelling skills.

Although we use alphabet letters to represent individual sounds, phonemic awareness has nothing to do with phonics. Phonemic awareness describes an ability to *hear* and *produce* the sounds in words, while phonics is a study of the relationship between printed letters and those spoken sounds. It is widely agreed that phonemic awareness abilities are an excellent predictor of learning to read

(Adams, 1990; IRA, 1998). However, phonological/phonemic awareness actually comprises a hierarchy of skills, with some preceding conventional reading, some developing concurrently with reading, and some acquired as a result of the ability to read.

Most children develop phonemic awareness easily and naturally just from living in a world of language. In fact, the joint position statement issued by the International Literacy Association (ILA) and the National Association for the Education of Young Children (NAEYC) reported that about 80 percent of children develop phonemic awareness without any explicit instruction at all (IRA, 1998). Many of the things we do at home and at school, such as reading rhyming texts and singing songs, help develop phonemic awareness simply by playing with the sounds of language. Some of the ways we can incidentally incorporate phonemic awareness into every part of the school day include:

- Singing songs and reading rhymes that manipulate the sounds in words, such as "*Willaby, Wallaby, Wennifer, an elephant sat on Jennifer*" or "*Dippety do dah, dippety day, My, oh, my, what a silly day!*"
- Playing word games, such as tongue twisters or rhyming riddles. *How do little cats keep their paws warm? With kitten mittens!*
- Using the children's names to reinforce letters and sounds (see Chapter 7). Reinforce syllables and sounds with name games such as "Let's play a game, tell me your name." When a child provides his/her name, the other children can clap the syllables, listen for sounds, and produce other words that begin or end with the same sound.
- Inviting students to listen for rhymes or words that begin the same way during read-alouds and shared reading. Choose books and poems that play with words, such as *Cock-a-doodle-MOO!* by Bernard Most, which describes a rooster's dismay when he loses his voice. The rooster enlists the aid of a cow to awaken the farm residents. Unable to say "cock-a-doodle-doo," the cow says, "mock-a-moodle-moo," "sock-a-noodle-moo," and other mixed-up versions of the morning greeting.
- Encouraging invented or phonetic spelling. The National Reading Panel (NICHD, 2000) reported that, even though phonemic awareness is an oral language skill, it is most effectively taught in conjunction with alphabet letters. Teaching students to stretch out words to hear all the sounds and to represent each sound with a letter helps reinforce both phonemic awareness and phonics. For more information on invented spelling, see "Bubble Gum Writing" in Chapter 6.

Invented spelling may very well be the best tool we have for reinforcing phonics and phonemic awareness.

For most children, these incidental experiences will be enough. That's why assessment is so critical. There's no point in wasting instructional time on phonemic awareness skills that students have already mastered. There are many diagnostic tools available that provide information about specific needs so that we can target instruction most effectively. Some children will require additional intervention in phonemic/phonological awareness, either because of learning difficulties or a lack of experience with language and print. For these children, identification, separation, and manipulation of sounds must be made explicit and practiced in ways that are both purposeful and playful, such as:

- *Specific routines to practice listening for sounds:* For example, record a collection of familiar sounds, such as horns honking, a person coughing, or a clock ticking. Have children close their eyes and try to identify the sound that they hear. Gradually add more sounds and have children identify them in order. This helps train them to listen for initial, medial, and final phonemes in words.

- *Sound sorting:* Provide a collection of small objects or picture cards for children to sort by initial sound, final sound, syllables, or rhymes. You can find a collection of picture cards for sorting at www.carlscorner.us.com/Sorts.htm
- *Elkonin boxes:* Developed by Russian psychologist Daniel Elkonin, this tool teaches children to segment sounds by moving a marker into a box for every sound that they hear. Marie Clay (1967) found that students who used Elkonin boxes were better able to hear sounds in words, sequence sounds, and connect sounds to letters.
- *Train sounds:* These help students understand the concepts of initial, medial, and final sounds in words. Use the Elkonin box routine, but instead of tokens, use magnetic toy train cars to reinforce engine (beginning), box car (middle), and caboose (ending). As well, the cars can be separated or "coupled" to reinforce segmenting and blending.

Vocabulary Development

The 30-Million-Word Gap!
Before they even begin school, children from professional homes have heard about 45 million words, whereas children from high poverty homes have heard only about 15 million words.
(Hart & Risley, 1995)

Most children learn about 600 root words per year from infancy throughout elementary school. But children of poverty enter school with far fewer words than their more advantaged peers. Even assuming all students make similar progress in vocabulary development, by Grade 5, the lowest students have only reached the level of an average second grader (Biemiller, 2003). Andrew Biemiller suggests that vocabulary deficits present by Grade 2 may account for differences throughout students' entire school careers. While it's important for all children to receive vocabulary instruction in early years, it's particulary imperative for children at risk, if they are to have success in reading and writing.

Michael Graves (2009) has identified these key elements of a strong vocabulary program:

- offering rich and varied language experiences through listening to stories and talking with one another,
- providing explicit teaching of individual words and word-learning strategies, and
- fostering awareness and interest in words through games and songs and word play.

Teaching Words

Where the Words Are
A typical children's storybook has more unique vocabulary than an average prime time television program!
(Hayes & Ahrens, 1988)

There is no formula for determining what words should be learned in Kindergarten. Isabel Beck and her colleagues (2002) defined three layers of vocabulary:

- Tier 1 words are basic core vocabulary, such as *table, said,* or *finger.*
- Tier 2 words are what we might consider "book language," the richer names for basic concepts, such as *crimson, strolled,* or *exclaimed.*
- Tier 3 words are technical vocabulary and usually have a very specific context, such as *chlorophyll, peninsula,* or *ecosystem.*

Most researchers recommend that words for instruction be chosen from Tier 2; however, many kindergartners will have already developed a significant content-area vocabulary and others will need explicit instruction in basic Tier 1 words as well. The teacher who knows his students well will be the best judge of what words can be taught.

Books are the best tools we have for teaching vocabulary. Exposing our Kindergarten children to a print-rich environment with many opportunities for shared reading and read-alouds helps to establish a foundation for strong vocabulary and other oral language skills. It's recommended that teachers define or explain challenging words as they read, and do their best to link the words to children's background knowledge. Particularly when it comes to English language learners, we mustn't take for granted that they will understand all the words, especially colloquial language.

But many researchers agree that read-alouds alone may not be enough (Beck, McKeown, & Kucan, 2002). A lot of children need direct and substantial vocabulary instruction in the early primary grades. The read-aloud is an excellent starting point for vocabulary instruction, but in order to make a word their own, children must understand how it sounds, how it looks, how it is used, and what it means, with multiple exposures in a variety of contexts.

Research-Based Models of Vocabulary Instruction

Most vocabulary strategies for young children involve harvesting words from pictures or books. In Emily Calhoun's (1999) Picture-Word Inductive Model, children "shake out" a collection of words from a picture. This collection of words is used to reinforce phonemic awareness, letter recognition, and letter–sound relationship practice. The words are sorted in a variety of ways, then used for guided and independent writing.

Isabel Beck's "Text Talk" (2002) is an analytic approach to vocabulary instruction, using vocabulary words from trade book read-alouds. A small number of key vocabulary words are selected for each story, based on the extent to which they are likely to be unfamiliar but potentially usable by young children. Children receive multiple exposures to each word, first in the context of the reading, then in a "child-friendly" definition, and finally in various extended experiences with the word, such as a visualization or a gesture.

Teach Three Words

An adaptation of the models described above, "Teach Three Words" involves explicitly teaching three key words from a read-aloud passage. The first challenge is selecting only three words. Choose words that the students are unlikely to know, but are likely to find interesting and usable, and that you will be able to define for the students in ways they will understand.

The acronym **MOVES** represents a routine for teaching and reinforcing new words, providing multiple experiences with the word before inviting students to "slip" it into their conversations. Here's an example using the word "tiptoe" from a Kindergarten read-aloud of *Somebody and the Three Blairs* by Marilyn Tolhurst:

- Start by introducing the word in the context of the reading. *(Remember how Somebody "tiptoed" into the house to sneak in?)*

Questions to ask when choosing focus words from a read-aloud:
- **Will my students find this word interesting?**
- **Will my students understand this word?**
- **Are my students likely to use this word?**

- *Meaning*: "*Tiptoeing is a way of walking on the tips of your toes, usually to be very quiet.*"
- *Other Contexts*: "*I might tiptoe through the wet grass so I don't get my feet wet.*"
- *Visual Cues*: Invite children to take a picture in their minds of someone tiptoeing.
- *Extend & Enrich the Experience*: *If you were walking past a sleeping baby, would you tiptoe or not? Stand on your tiptoes for yes and on your flat feet for no. If you were marching in a band, would you tiptoe or not? Tell your partner about another time when you might tiptoe.*
- *Slip It into Conversation*: Post the word card in a visible spot and make a tally mark any time anyone uses, sees, or hears the word in the classroom.

Storm and Sort, List and Label

Early literacy expert Susan Newman (2011) has said that learning words in categories is a "bootstrap" to further learning. When children brainstorm words to fit categories, such as "things that are square," "things that have buttons," or "containers for holding things," they are creating schema into which many, many more words can be added over time.

You and your students can generate word lists from pictures, read-alouds, or shared reading to sort in many different ways. For example, find an interesting photograph and enlarge it as much as possible. Then, invite the children to suggest words inspired by the picture. Write each word on a card or sticky note, along with the name of the child who suggested it, and attach it to the picture. Tell the children that they will "own" these words to help the rest of the students remember them. In this way, children who are not yet reading conventionally can still participate in sorting and other activities with the words. You'll have to be the judge of how many words your group can work with at a time.

If your students are unfamiliar with sorting, you might want to start with a closed sort, in which the categories are predefined. For example, you might ask children to find all the words with one, two, or three syllables. On another day, you might ask the students, "What word on our picture goes with *box*?" They might suggest *crate* or *basket*; in which case, you could prompt them with, "These are all words that tell about…." If a student suggests something like *apple goes with box*, ask him to explain why. Always ask students to justify their responses and accept any response that is reasonably explained.

Shared reading formats, such as posters, poems, and Big Books, can also be excellent vocabulary sources for sorting. "**Dump, Clump, and Plump**" is one routine for vocabulary sorting.

1. **Dump** out a group of words from a picture, read-aloud, or shared reading text.
2. Invite students to **clump** the words into groups and give each group a name or label.
3. Extend the experience by asking students to **plump** up their groups with more words of their own for each category. As a further extension, you might invite students to come up with additional related words such as synonyms, antonyms, or modifiers.

Some Rules for Sorting
- Every word must fit into at least one category.
- There must be at least two words in every category.
- Some words may fit into more than one category.
- Each category should have a name or label.

Word Warm-ups

Sometimes it's hard to find time in the day to fit in explicit oral language instruction and practice. So, why not make a five- to ten-minute "word warm-up" part of each day's morning meeting? These engaging routines are both playful and purposeful, establishing a context for a day full of rich talk and powerful learning. Of course, these routines don't always need to take place at a structured time of day or even with the whole class; they can be used as five-minute fillers before home-time, after lunch, or during outdoor activity.

Mystery Monday involves some sort of guessing games, usually requiring the students to ask or answer questions. For example, here's a variation on the traditional "show and tell" routine: Provide a gift bag so students can take turns bringing a mystery item from home. The other students must ask "yes/no" questions for the leader to answer as they try to guess what's in the bag. Note that it's important to model and practice asking and answering questions to make this activity truly effective. And for some students, the teacher might need to keep a collection of mystery items on hand.

Twos-Day Tuesday focuses on pairs of words: rhymes, synonyms, antonyms, compounds, etc. Riddles like "hinky-pinkies" ask questions which must be answered with a pair of rhyming words (such as "What can you give a hog without any hair? A pig wig!").

WOW Words Wednesday presents interesting new vocabulary. It might be the day when we "teach three words" or we might talk about color words, size words, words that show beauty, or words that describe movement.

Thinking Thursday requires students to brainstorm, categorize, analyze, or reason in some way. They might have to work in pairs to generate words for "things that have buttons" or to group words in a list by common attributes.

Funny Friday is a day to play with word sounds. Sing songs, read books, or recite rhymes that manipulate sounds, such as "Down by the Bay" ("Did you ever see a whale with a polka-dot tail?") or "I Like to Eat Apples and Bananas," in which each verse is sung with a different vowel sound ("Oh loke to ote opples and bono-nos").

In his book, *Reading Begins at Birth*, David Doake states, "In order to learn to read as fluently and easily as they learn to talk, children have to establish control over the oral dimensions of written language" (1988, 30). Taking time each day for both explicit and implicit oral language will lay the foundation for future success in learning to read and write.

4

Reading to and by Children

The storybook read-aloud has been a mainstay in Kindergarten classrooms for as long as there have been Kindergarten classrooms. We read aloud to expose children to new vocabulary and to the fluency and flow of language. We read aloud to spark inquiry and to help children find answers to their questions. And we read aloud to teach children about the wider world and to instill a love of literacy. Over 30 years ago, the U.S. Commission on Reading asserted, "The single most important activity for building the knowledge required for eventual success in reading is reading aloud to children" (Anderson et al., 1985, 23). That statement is every bit as true today.

Reading aloud also contributes to improved comprehension. Story reading, more than any other activity, provides children with information about the processes and functions of written language in a meaningful, holistic context, instead of as isolated subskills. Through carefully planned read-alouds, children learn to apply their background knowledge, their understanding of how stories work, and their personal reactions in order to construct meaning from reading.

In spite of the many merits of reading aloud, however, simply immersing children in books will not necessarily turn them into readers. If we want our read-aloud program to support reading development, we need to select quality texts that extend children's knowledge of literature, language, and the world; we need to read and reread those texts; and we need to make the children active participants in the reading process.

Three Keys to an Effective Classroom Read-Aloud
- **Selecting rich literature and nonfiction**
- **Making children active participants in the reading process**
- **Rereading familiar texts**

Selecting Books for a Read-Aloud Program

Given the sheer quantity of excellent children's books available today, perhaps the biggest challenge for teachers is choosing what books to read. Choose books you love—because your students will love them too. The interactive read-aloud is not the place for simple, predictable, repetitive texts that lend little to growth in vocabulary, background knowledge, or comprehension. When choosing fiction for young children, consider the following criteria:

- **Finding topics that children can relate to, but that also extend their background knowledge.** Familiar situations with an unusual twist enable readers to connect what they already know to new ideas.
- **Characters that are clearly defined and few in number, preferably containing one main character with whom children can identify.** Young readers generally prefer characters, whether human or animal, that think, act, and talk like children.

- Fast-moving plots that are logically sequenced, with a realistic problem and a satisfying resolution.
- A theme or message that is subtle but appropriate to the world of four-to-six-year-olds.
- Language that extends children's range of vocabulary and syntax.
- Illustrations that don't just enhance the text but also enrich it.

Children need to see their own lives reflected in the books that are read. In our increasingly diverse society, it's more important than ever to fill our children's worlds with books that reflect a range of faces, cultures, beliefs, and lifestyles. We need to honor the lives of all our children and teach them to appreciate both the differences and the similarities of the lives of those around them. In selecting multicultural literature, we look for books that are accurate and authentic and that avoid stereotypes in either text or illustrations. Take care: even a positive stereotype (e.g., "Canadians are so polite") is still a stereotype.

Nonfiction Texts

Our kindergartners thrive on "story," but facts and information are equally important. In fact, Nell Duke (2004) suggests that our primary reading programs should consist of one-third fictional texts, one-third informational texts, and one-third functional texts (the kind we read to function in the world, such as schedules, brochures, labels, advertisements, and street signs). In the past, there weren't many nonfiction texts appropriate for Kindergarten; today, however, many beautifully crafted informational books for young children can be found to match any subject or interest. Some considerations for choosing nonfiction read-alouds include the following:

- Current and factually accurate information
- Illustrations, especially photographs, that accurately portray the action, mood, and intent of the material
- Text with interesting and engaging style and voice

Info-text is not the only form of nonfiction that is suitable for children. Consider picture book biographies, procedural and how-to texts, and even persuasive texts, such as *Should There Be Zoos?* (Stead, 2002). Of course, read-alouds do not all need to be in book form. Magazines, brochures, and even newspapers can be sources of nonfiction reading. And let's not forget reading from the world-wide web. In one of Donna-Lynn's schools, the Kindergarten teachers created QR (Quick Response) Codes in discovery centres for children to look up more information on topics of interest. A QR Code is a mobile-phone-readable bar code that can store website addresses and other information. The children hold up a tablet to the symbol and it automatically links them to a website with more information on the topic.

A final note on book selection: Be cautious about texts that combine fiction and nonfiction, such as The Magic School Bus series by Joanna Cole and Bruce Degen or *Diary of a Worm* and other similar titles by Doreen Cronin. These books can be delightful read-alouds, but they will require more special attention when helping students distinguish between the facts and the story.

How to Read Aloud

What We Think We Know

As a reading tool for nonfiction, Lori likes to use a modification of the RAN Chart developed by Tony Stead (2006). Fold a sheet of chart paper in half, like a book. The front of the folder is labeled "What We Think We Know," the two sections of the inside are labeled "We Were Right!" and "What We Learned," and the back is labeled "What We Still Wonder."

Before reading, invite the students to tell anything they *think* they know about the topic and record *all* their ideas on sticky notes. (Alternatively, children might be invited to write or draw their own ideas.) Each sticky note is attached to the "What We Think We Know" section of the folder. (Anyone who has had a kindergartner inform them in no uncertain terms, "Penguins can dance because I saw it on the movie," will agree that it's dangerous to treat these statements as facts!)

After reading, we go back and look for "What We Think We Know" facts that were confirmed by what we read. These stickies are moved to the inside of the folder under the heading "We Were Right!" We also record any new facts that were learned and place those sticky notes in the "What We Learned" section of the book.

Sometimes questions or "wonderings" about the topic are more focused if we generate them *after* reading, so we record our questions on stickies and post them at the back of the book in the "What We Still Wonder" section. If children find the answers to the questions, they can write them on stickies and add them to this page as well.

In addition to activating prior knowledge, the "What We Think We Know" folder sets a purpose for reading—to find out what facts are confirmed in the text and what new facts we will learn. After reading, we can use the "We Were Right!" and "What We Learned" facts for a variety of purposes, including sorting, vocabulary development, and interactive writing.

Most of us don't spend a lot of time planning our read-alouds. After all, there isn't a *wrong* way to read aloud, is there? But there are things we can do to make the classroom read-aloud program more purposeful and engaging for our students. Here are some elements of an instructionally effective read-aloud:

- Choosing rich texts that engage the students' interests, build background knowledge, and increase vocabulary
- Modeling expressive, fluent oral reading, and thinking aloud during reading
- Explaining difficult concepts and complex vocabulary
- Activating students' background knowledge and guiding them in applying it to understanding the text
- Reading interactively, pausing strategically for discussion and comprehension
- Supporting oral-language development and higher-level thinking through guided discussion and "TTYN" (talk to your neighbor)
- Revisiting familiar text to build comprehension and fluency

Effective storybook reading is an interactive process. Too often, we don't allow children to interact with the text while it is being read, insisting that they hold their comments until after the reading is done. And yet, encouraging students to respond during reading enhances both comprehension and engagement with the text. When we pause to confirm predictions, ask questions, and draw inferences, we are teaching children that making meaning from text is an active process that occurs all through the reading.

Talking about text has been extensively linked to greater literacy growth; however, it is *analytic* talk that really makes a difference. We know that children engage more deeply with reading when they are invited to ask questions, support predictions, make judgments, and offer personal responses. But teaching young children to engage in analytic talk requires skillful modeling as well as encouraging, prompting, scaffolding, and probing them to dig deeper into the text. That's why teachers frequently comment, think aloud, share our own responses, and clarify information and vocabulary as we read.

There is great value in revisiting a book two, three, and even more times (IRA/NAEYC, 1998). Research consistently supports rereading texts for building comprehension and vocabulary. Even in Kindergarten, a rich read-aloud will present new insights to be gained from each reading. Children comprehend and respond more deeply to books that have been read previously. Miriam Martinez and Nancy Roser (1985) found that not only did children make more comments and connections while rereading familiar texts, but the responses were more rich, varied, and complex. Rereading benefits all students, but appears to be particularly important for our most vulnerable children (Morrow, O'Connor, & Smith, 1990).

Planning an Interactive Read-Aloud Sequence

"Effective interactive read-alouds include a systematic approach that incorporates teachers' modeling of higher level thinking, asking thoughtful questions calling for analytic talk, and prompting children to recall a story in some way." (McGee & Schickedanz, 2007, 11)

Some teachers fear that making the read-aloud interactive will turn it into a free-for-all in which students lose the thread of the story entirely. That's why it's important to carefully plan each read-aloud session to include intentional "pause points" and prompts to model thinking and focus discussion. Rather than distracting the students, these interactions enrich experiences with the text, because the students become active participants in constructing meaning from the reading. Lea McGee and Judith Schickedanz (2007) suggest that texts be read aloud three times for deeper comprehension and engagement. And let's not forget that the read-aloud need not involve the whole class or even a whole book for that matter. Small groups often lend themselves to richer conversations about the reading. And revisiting short excerpts can serve specific learning goals.

Although not every read-aloud will be equally intensive, the following "Three Day Read-Aloud Sequence" invites purposeful, repeated reading to build comprehension and encourage analytic talk.

Three Day Read-Aloud Sequence

DAY ONE: "TESTING THE WATERS"

- Start with a "Three Ps" book introduction: Preview the text, activate Prior knowledge, and set a Purpose for the reading (what the children will learn or what strategies they will apply). The "What We Think We Know" Box (page 47) is a good tool for a nonfiction book introduction.
- Read with fluency, phrasing, and expression. As you read, model your own responses to the story. Pause occasionally to revisit predictions, to express curiosity or confusion, or to comment on something you found interesting.

Be sure to explain ideas or words you think the students might not understand. It's a good idea to prepare ahead and tab these pause points with sticky notes.

- Plan for three or four selected pause points for partner-talk. Keep these interactions short (a minute or two) and focused (e.g., predicting, anticipating, inferring) by providing a prompt or question. It's not necessary for students to share their thinking with the whole group, but you will want to eavesdrop on the conversations to assess students' thinking and comprehension. Keep a notebook or tablet on hand to record students' ideas to revisit later.

- After reading, invite a general response to the reading and a "big idea" question.

DAY TWO: "DIVING DEEPER"

Partner talk is a powerful opportunity for children to articulate their thinking in a safe and supported setting. When children must turn to a partner, they are more likely to have their share of "talk time" and less likely to hide behind more assertive classmates.

- Reread the text with more frequent pause points, to prompt deeper thinking, and encourage student responses and questions. You might even stop on every page if the children want to say something about them.

- Focus on some specific comprehension work (such as drawing inferences or learning about characters). Prompt or question students to encourage analytic talk.

- After reading, engage children in some retelling games and activities (see below).

- Explicitly teach two or three vocabulary words (see page 41).

DAY THREE: "DIPPING BACK IN"

- Reread the text with pauses as warranted by student observations and questions.

- Invite students to join in the reading, as appropriate. (e.g., "You can't catch me! I'm the gingerbread man!")

- Examine specific aspects of style, craft, illustrations, and language.

- Allow for individual responses (talking, drawing, writing).

After Reading

Retelling Ropes: Manipulatives such as retelling ropes help children recall the elements of a story as they touch each object on the rope. Cut a length of wide ribbon or thick braided rope (about 40 cm or 16 inches) for each retelling rope. Attach clip-art images that represent different story elements, such as a person for characters and a house for setting. Tie a knot in the rope to represent the problem of the story. String colored beads on the rope to represent the beginning (green), middle (yellow), and end (red) of the story. Tie a bow on the end of the rope to represent the way the problem was solved and the story was "tied up."

In the past, many of us have felt compelled to plan some sort of activity to follow-up or extend the reading. However, not all books lend themselves to cooking or crafts. After-reading routines should develop naturally from the text and help to make our students better readers, writers, and thinkers.

Retelling is an effective tool for assessing and enhancing comprehension, as well as laying the foundation for future competencies, such as summarizing (Gambrell & Dromsky, 2000). It requires children to think about story structure, distinguish main ideas, and use the language of the story. However, it's important to explicitly teach students how to retell a story or a collection of facts. For example, many children need to be taught the concept of beginning–middle–end, to name and define characters, and to distinguish key events. As children are learning to retell, scaffold them by starting the story and inviting them to continue it. Prompt the students if they falter or get off track. Even prompts like, "Tell me more" or "Then what happened?" can generate more detail. Sometimes holding a visual aid, such as a puppet or toy related to the story or a retelling rope as described in the box above, can trigger reminders of the text.

Individual writing (or drawing) in response to reading has been shown to support comprehension and retention, from Kindergarten through to college (Graham & Hebert, 2010). Shared and interactive writing experiences are other ways to respond to a read-aloud. Topics or themes from the read-aloud may be springboards for new writing pieces, or "text innovations" may be created based on a pattern or structure in the book.

Story Souvenirs

Make the home-school reading connection (and build long-term memory) by sending home "souvenirs" of classroom read-alouds. These souvenirs might be pencil toppers, dollar store items, or even clip-art pictures to remind the children to retell the story to their caregivers. Use your classroom blog or email communication to remind parents to look for these souvenirs and provide a summary of the story along with any questions the students might ask.

Always make the books available to students after a read-aloud; these are the texts children are most likely to choose for independent reading. Displaying these featured books on a picture stand reminds students to revisit these old friends. Imaginative play and creative drama will emerge naturally from reading experiences, especially when prompted by a copy of the book and a collection of props in the reading corner. Jodi Welsch (2008) found that when her students were provided with some simple costumes and props, children engaged in both "play within text," consisting of close re-enactments of the stories, and "play beyond text," that involved using some element of character, plot, or dialogue in a new story.

Reading aloud can be an important way to develop skilled and engaged readers. Children learn about the language of books and the structure of story. They gain access to new and complex concepts, creating background knowledge on which to build further learning. And, through sensitive scaffolding of children's questions and conversations, we can bridge even the youngest students to higher levels of thinking, communicating, and responding to text.

Reading by Children

It's never too early to begin fostering independent reading habits. We know that the amount of leisure time spent reading is an excellent predictor of and a causal factor in older students' growth in reading and vocabulary (Fielding et al., 1986). Right from Kindergarten, children who read more perform better on literacy assessments and on measures of general knowledge (Lapp, Flood, & Roser, 2000). However, independent reading in Kindergarten is not like independent reading in upper grades.

Most children aren't reading conventionally when they first enter Kindergarten; however, they do interact with books in a variety of ways. In Elizabeth Sulzby's classic 1985 study, she noted that children go through a set of predictable stages in their ability to acquire stories from books. Long before they can actually decode the words, many children engage in role-play reading, turning pages of a book and telling the story using familiar expressions such as "once upon a time" or "happily ever after." As they begin to understand the phonetic principle, some children refuse to read at all, because they "don't know how." Eventually, however, the children build a repertoire of sight words and decoding strategies that enable them to be conventional readers.

As with all classroom activities, it's important to establish routines and clarify expectations for children during independent reading time. We model the appropriate behaviors and collaboratively construct an anchor chart that describes what independent reading looks and sounds like. Early in the school year, Lori teaches "Three Ways to Read in Kindergarten," based on Sulzby's research. She models, explicitly demonstrates, and guides the children as they practice "reading the pictures" (browsing through the illustrations), making up their own stories, or actually decoding the print. They learn that different texts require different types of reading. An important lesson for children to learn is that readers "talk to their brains" about the pictures, stories, and words in a book. This self-talk creates an important foundation for self-monitoring comprehension.

Three Ways to Read in Kindergarten

1. **Read the pictures.**
2. **Make up your own story.**
3. **Read the words.**

The Classroom Reading Collection

What makes a classroom where children choose to read independently? An attractive and accessible classroom library, according to Leslie Morrow (2003). The reading corner is the focal point of many Kindergarten classrooms, often doubling as a gathering place for morning meetings, read-alouds, modeled writing, and other large-group activities. Soft cushions, private nooks and crannies, and plenty of books of all types and genres make the reading corner a desirable spot for free choice activity. Scour yard sales for an old upholstered chair or sofa and ask for carpet remnants at flooring stores. If possible, place the reading corner near a window where there will be plenty of natural light or place lamps nearby for ambient lighting. Try to find ways to create private spaces; for example, a packing box from a new appliance makes a great book nook. You might even be able to enlist the assistance of a talented volunteer to build a reading loft or sew beanbag chairs or oversize pillows for the students to sit on. Inviting reading corners contain anything from tents to bunk beds to electric fireplaces. Add some literature-based dramatic play props, such as puppets, costumes, and dolls, and you'll have a reading corner that the children won't be able to resist.

Leslie Morrow also recommends that the classroom library contain eight to ten books per student. Research has shown that children who have access to books in the classroom read up to 50 percent more than students in classrooms without libraries (Bissett, 1969). Miriam Martinez and William Teale (1988) found that emergent readers are more likely to choose books that are predictable and familiar to them. In fact, they reported that the books Kindergarten children are most likely to try to read conventionally are the ones that have been read and reread

In some communities, it's possible to get a special public library card for educators. Either the teacher or a volunteer can sign out a collection of books and exchange them each month. Keep these books in a special place (such as an open suitcase) so students know where to return them.

during shared reading. Any time you read a book aloud, place it in the reading corner for students to visit again. A rule of thumb is to change about one-third of the books each month, though special favorites may be kept on display longer, even for the entire year.

Walk into any bookstore and you are likely to notice many marketing tricks for attracting consumers to the books: an organizational structure that is easy to navigate, books organized by theme or author, special displays that are changed regularly, and featured books with covers facing out. The same display techniques may be applied to our Kindergarten libraries. Books in the classroom collection should be stored within easy reach of students, with covers visible. One clever way to display books is in plastic rain gutters mounted low on the classroom walls. However, not all the books in the Kindergarten library need to be in one place. Strategically placing reading materials around the room helps to ensure that students will be encountering print all day long.

What Kinds of Books Do Kindergarten Children Read?

Choice is a key to engaging any readers, and kindergartners are no exception. The reading materials in the classroom library should represent a range of genres, including stories, poetry, informational texts, Big Books, folk and fairy tales, and class and student-made books. Children enjoy revisiting books that have been read in the classroom. They take delight in class-made books to which they've contributed. It's very important for young children to see their lives reflected in the books they read; be sure to include a range of cultures and family structures in the collection.

Trade books (those published and sold for general use, as opposed to educational books) often have interesting story lines, beautiful illustrations, and rich language, but these books are usually too difficult for emerging readers to read independently. Leveled books, usually "little books," are designed specifically to support growing readers at various stages of development, but they do little to enrich a child's imagination or background knowledge. However, there is room in our Kindergarten library for both.

The practice of leveling texts was originally developed by Marie Clay (1991) to provide reading materials of graduated difficulty for Reading Recovery™ intervention. Today, these little books are ubiquitous in primary classrooms as tools for small group reading instruction and practice. We need to ensure that students have a range of types and levels of books at their disposal to help them develop the very important life skill of choosing books they *can* and *want to* read. Says Kathy Collins, "I worry that if our kids are limited to just-right books 100 percent of the time in our classrooms, they may not learn the possibilities and promise of reading, nor will they easily develop their own goals and plans as readers that are more personal than moving to the next reading level" (2008, 72).

We're not suggesting that teachers prevent students from reading "just-right" books during independent reading time. But maybe it's time to expand our definition of just-right books for independent reading to include more challenging books that capture students' interest and engagement even if they can't read all the words. On the other hand, for many youngsters, it's incredibly empowering to be able to select books in which they can read conventionally. Why not make leveled books *available* to students for self-selected reading, but not *limit* students to reading books at their independent or instructional reading level? A

"Just-right" texts might range from books at a student's independent reading level to those that the student is particularly interested in browsing.

box of books at various levels might be made available along with trade books for student self-selection.

Individual Book Boxes are one way to ensure that every child has a collection of reading materials at his or her fingertips at all times—and can use reading time for reading rather than choosing books. Cardboard or plastic magazine storage boxes work well for individual book boxes, as they hold a range of book sizes and store neatly on a shelf. In each student's book box, there might be some leveled guided reading texts as well as a collection of trade books that the child has chosen herself. The book box might also contain a folder of class poems that have been read together during shared reading and even some little books that the child has written herself. At the beginning of the year, the teacher can provide strong guidance and might even choose the books for the children's book boxes, but, over the course of the year, we want to gradually release responsibility to the students to select their own books. The materials in these book boxes may be changed on schedule or spontaneously, depending on the students, the teacher, and the classroom routines.

In some classrooms where "read to yourself" is an independent learning option during the reading block, teachers may feel compelled (or mandated) to limit student reading to books that support children's abilities to build decoding skills. In this case, it would be useful to schedule another part of the day for self-selected reading. Perhaps you can squeeze in some "library" periods each week. Some teachers invite children to read when they first arrive at school in the morning; others find "rest and read" an effective transition after recess or outdoor play. One advantage to scheduling independent reading times separately from small-group teaching time is the teacher is free to circulate among the students to make observations and assessments, and to take a few minutes to confer with students about what they are reading.

Of course, we need to accept that what is referred to as "Uninterrupted Sustained Silent Reading" in other grades is rarely uninterrupted, silent, or even conventional "reading" in Kindergarten! Kindergarten children need to hear their voices saying the words in the books. They generally can't sustain attention to books for very long. That's why we build routines such as reading in whisper voices and gradually increasing reading stamina. Sharing a book with a buddy, talking about reading, and browsing pictures are all part of Kindergarten book time.

Teaching any routine, including independent reading, takes time and patience. Allow plenty of time for modeling, demonstration, and guided practice before expecting children to function independently. Patience will pay off in a smoothly flowing independent reading program that supports children in becoming readers and lovers of books.

Home-Reading Programs

A discussion of independent reading wouldn't be complete without mentioning the home-school connection. When parents are on board with the reading program, the children get much-needed additional reading practice and see reading as an activity that extends beyond school. Even Mom and Dad read (we hope). A take-home reading program that extends the reading experience beyond the classroom helps children to see literacy as part of their whole lives.

What is referred to as Uninterrupted Sustained Silent Reading in upper grades is rarely uninterrupted, sustained, silent, or even actual reading in Kindergarten.

We need to remember that parents are not teachers. They might not have the knowledge to support children in word-solving beyond "sound it out," or they might not read English at all. That's why it's important that books for take-home reading practice are already familiar to the children. Parent volunteers or upper grade reading buddies might be trained to help kindergartners choose books for home reading and to practice reading the books with them before the books are sent home. For children who do not get reading support at home, these reading buddies can provide a listening ear.

Some teachers are reluctant to initiate home-reading programs because they are concerned that the books will not return to school. Some checks and balances, such as carding the take-home books and not permitting students to take home another book until the previous one has been returned, can help mitigate loss. However, it often seems that the child who needs the reading practice most is the one least likely to return his or her books expediently. Surely we can find some way to support these little readers, even if it means losing a few books. One alternative is to send home reproducible books from websites such as www.readinga-z.com or www.dltk-teach.com/minibooks/index.htm.

Not every family has access to reading materials, so some teachers prepare special Read-Aloud Book Bags. These bags generally contain one or two picture books, along with an artifact or hands-on activity, such as a stuffed animal, instructions and materials for a craft, or a game to play. A guide might also be included to help caregivers talk with the children about the book or take part in the accompanying activity.

Of course, the best home-reading activity for young children is caregivers reading or telling stories to them. Parents are encouraged to share stories that honor their own family's native culture and language. It takes a village to raise a reader, and involving families in supporting literacy development benefits everyone.

5

Shared and Guided Reading: The "We Do" of Reading Instruction

The interactive read-aloud is a wonderful vehicle for modeling and demonstrating the reading process, but we also need to provide opportunities for children to access print themselves. Shared reading and guided reading enable teachers to support and scaffold young readers as they navigate letters and sounds. They are the "we do" of the gradual release of responsibility.

Read-aloud	Shared Reading	Guided Reading
• May be large group or small group • Uses rich texts beyond the individual reading levels of the students • Multilevel, to allow learning from all students • Teacher-directed	• May be large group or small group • Uses engaging texts somewhat beyond the levels of the students and enlarged for all to see • Multilevel to offer something for everyone to learn • Teacher-led, with students joining in	• Small, needs-based group • Uses texts carefully selected to be at an accessible reading level for the students in the group • Targeted to the specific needs of the group • Student-centred, with teacher support

Shared Reading

It seems that some children learn to read almost magically, just by being read to. Yet Dolores Durkin's (1966) classic research showed that most children who came to school reading had already experienced much incidental instruction from parents. When parents and children cuddle together to read a book, they usually talk about the story and the pictures. They share their reactions and recite familiar passages together. They may even point out letters and words. These interactions with text create a solid foundation for learning to read.

Unfortunately, even the most generous lap can't hold 20 students or more. So how can we replicate the benefits of the bedtime story in a school setting? Four decades ago, Don Holdaway (1979) and his colleagues in New Zealand created what they called the "shared book experience." By enlarging text to make it visible to groups of children, they could provide the read-aloud experience and, at the same time, draw children's attention to concepts about print and letter knowledge. The shared reading experience is intended, first and foremost, to provide a joyful reading experience and motivate children to become readers themselves. But shared reading also offers opportunities for systematic and explicit instruction in the reading process. This is what distinguishes shared reading from the traditional read-aloud.

Shared reading experiences benefit Kindergarten students by helping them:

- Take pleasure in reading.
- Engage with text that is too difficult for them to read independently.
- Develop concepts about print and phonological awareness.
- Build phonetic skills in the context of connected text.
- Learn to use meaning, structure, and visual cues to monitor and self-correct.
- Identify high-frequency words.
- Build comprehension strategies such as predicting and connecting to prior knowledge.
- Learn to identify and understand text features and story text structures.
- Think, act, and see themselves as readers.

Shared reading takes many forms in the Kindergarten classroom, from Big Books to language experience charts to print projected on a screen. Regardless of the medium, there are certain common elements to the shared-book experience:

- enlarged print and illustrations visible to all
- modeled reading by a teacher or more experienced reader
- repeated readings to focus on comprehension, fluency, and print features

During a shared-book experience, students first observe, then gradually join in during multiple readings of a text. The first reading usually focuses on comprehension and appreciation of the text, as the teacher models expressive oral reading, sometimes thinking aloud about his own reading processes or responses to the text. Subsequent readings are used to draw students' attention to the print and how it works. The teacher employs techniques such as tracking the print, pointing out spaces between words, or highlighting graphophonic elements, such as initial sounds or letter patterns. The text is read several times, with students gradually taking over from the teacher as they become comfortable and familiar with the text.

Shared reading lessons are designed to be fast-paced and interactive, offering something for every child in the group to learn. They should also be short; just ten minutes a day is enough.

Choosing Texts for Shared Reading

When working with large groups or the whole class, it's important that lessons be:
- **Brief**
- **Intentional**
- **Multilevel**

Big Books, charts, and posters are the traditional media for shared reading. But with today's technology, interactive whiteboards, document projectors, and even the lowly overhead projector can be used to enlarge a piece of text. However, not just any piece of enlarged text will be effective for shared reading.

Too many Big Books have too much print on the page and are too complicated for shared-book routines. For example, it's easy to find Big Book versions of such favorites as *Chrysanthemum* by Kevin Henkes or *The Paper Bag Princess* by Robert Munsch. Although they are wonderful read-alouds, these texts are simply not suited to shared reading because of the challenging vocabulary and density of print. Young readers are unlikely to be able to join in the reading, no matter how many times the text is revisited. When choosing commercial Big Books for shared reading in Kindergarten, look for books with simple, repetitive language and just a few lines of text on each page, but with rich enough content to be worth reading over and over.

Brenda Parkes (2000), the author of many books written especially for shared reading, recommends the following considerations:

- clear, readable print with ample space between words and lines
- rich, memorable language
- a strong, satisfying storyline with a predictable structure
- bright, vigorous illustrations that support the text

Published Big Books are often costly, but the classroom library can be supplemented with student- and teacher-made books. Traditional rhymes, chants, and songs make excellent charts or illustrated books. You can word-process the text, enlarging the font to a readable size (at least 24 points), and add clip art or student illustrations to create your own Big Books.

Shared Reading with Big Books

Big Books are often trade books printed in an enlarged format, although some are created specifically to be Big Books. Shared reading of Big Books enables the teacher to model and demonstrate reading processes using full-length stories and nonfiction texts.

The "Show What You Know" Game invites students to point out elements of print and pictures that they recognize from the cover of the book, honoring what each child brings to the reading experience.

The shared book experience begins much like the interactive read-aloud, described in Chapter 4. We start with a "Three Ps" book introduction: preview the text, activate prior knowledge, and set a purpose for reading. The book preview might be as simple as a one-sentence overview of the main idea, or as elaborate as a picture walk through the entire book. Often, we play the "Show What You Know" game. This involves displaying the cover of the book without reading the title and inviting individual students to point out pictures, letters, and words that they recognize. Everyone's contribution is honored, from the child who can identify only a letter or two to the child who can read whole words or the entire title.

Establish predetermined "pause points" during which students are invited to turn and talk with a partner about what they are thinking or wondering.

During the first reading of the Big Book, the teacher reads aloud, pausing occasionally to comment or reflect. He will stop at a couple of predetermined pause points for students to turn and talk about a specific question or strategy (such as "What are you wondering right now?" or "What do you predict is going to happen next?"). This initial exposure to the book focuses on overall comprehension and an aesthetic response to the content.

On subsequent readings, we begin to focus on letters and words. As the children become more familiar with the text, they join in on reading familiar parts, especially those that are repeated. This activity builds fluency by encouraging students to read chorally and encourages students to connect what they see on the page to what they say and hear. We might also include a vocabulary focus, such as "Teach Three Words," described in Chapter 3. There are several playful but purposeful activities that students can engage in as they focus on print features:

- Be a detective and hunt for specific letters, words, and text features.
- Cover a word with a sticky note and have the students guess the word.
- Highlight specific words or letters with removable highlighting tape.
- Underline or circle words or letters with waxed string (known commercially as Wikki Stix™).

Reading Tools from the Dollar Store
Each rereading is a new experience when we use different pointers and framers each time.
- **Anything with a point may be used for tracking, such as: magic wands, cocktail swizzle sticks, chopsticks, pointers, or bubble wands.**
- **Anything with a hole may be used for framing words, such as: tracing toys, magnifying glasses or fly swatters with holes cut in the centre, the centre of plastic letters, such as O or D, toy bracelets, rings, or even glasses without lenses.**

Reading "manipulatives" such as trackers and framers keep kids interested as we go back into the text repeatedly for different purposes. Many inexpensive items for tracking or framing print may be found at your local dollar store (see sidebar).

Simple tools like these add fun, variety, and interest to word study. They make each reading a new adventure. But nothing compares to the empowerment kindergartners feel when they can actually read the words on the page.

After reading, we may retell the story or engage in an interactive writing experience. Shared or interactive writing routines often involve creating a new piece of writing based on the theme, pattern, or text features of the book used for shared reading. For example, a class might create books like "Children, Children, What Do You See?" (based on *Brown Bear, Brown Bear* by Bill Martin, Jr.) or "Harry the Hamster's Week" (based on *Cookie's Week* by Cindy Ward). Other shared or interactive writing experiences from shared reading might include the following:

- summarizing or retelling what happened in the text
- writing a letter to or from a character
- creating another story with a character in the book
- writing their own "all about" books on a related topic
- recreating part of the story in a different form, such as "how-to"
- acting out the story using props

The final step in the shared reading process is to place the book in the reading area for students to access on their own. Miriam Martinez and William Teale (1988) found that, of all the books in the classroom library, children are most likely to try to read conventionally from the Big Books that have been read in class. Unfortunately however, these books often become so well-loved that they begin to fall apart, so it's important to reinforce with the children how to take care of the books.

Shared Reading Using Interactive Charts

Play "I Spy" Games with Experience Charts
I spy with my little eye…
- **a word that starts the same as** *David*
- **a word that has twin letters**
- **a word that has an** *s*
- **a word with three syllables**
- **a word that rhymes with** *ball*
- **a word that starts with an upper-case letter**

Language experience charts enable children to see their talk written down. This process of scribing the children's ideas is known as "shared writing," described more fully in Chapter 6. While the teacher writes, she explains the process of transcribing spoken words into print, such as stretching out words, inserting spaces between words, or adding capitals and punctuation. Experience charts may serve a range of topics and purposes, from class news to reading responses to documenting the changes in the classroom amaryllis plant as it grows.

Experience charts are a wonderful medium for shared reading activities. Because this writing uses their own words and is connected to their own lives, emergent readers are much quicker to read and remember it. The charts may be revisited over and over, each time focusing on different aspects of the print.

> **Popcorn, Popcorn, Yum, yum, yum,**
> **Don't you wish that you had some?**
> Invite students to offer ideas for words to replace "popcorn." Write their suggestions on word cards and read the text with the new ideas in place. Clap out syllables in words: pop-corn, ta-co, pep-per-o-ni, cha-pa-ti. Have the chart and manipulatives available for students to work with independently throughout the day.

An experience chart can also be reassembled into a class Big Book. Cut the chart into individual lines and give each child his or her own line. (Some children might be asked to cut their lines into individual words, then reassemble them like a jigsaw puzzle.) The children can glue their lines to large pieces of paper and add illustrations. These pages may be laminated for durability and coil bound into a Big Book, which is guaranteed to be a popular item in the classroom library.

Interactive charts are created by adapting an enlarged poem, song, or finger play so that the children can substitute words and phrases of their own. For example, in the nursery rhyme, "Jack be nimble, Jack be quick, Jack jump over the candlestick," the name can be changed each time: "Diego be nimble, Diego be quick…." In a song like "Old McDonald Had a Farm," children can substitute different animals and their corresponding sounds. This affords many opportunities for developing phonological awareness, such as counting syllables, rhyming words, or matching sounds.

The easiest way to facilitate this kind of manipulation of text is to use an interactive white board. But there are also ways that a paper chart can be adapted for manipulation, such as:

- Attaching paper fasteners to the chart so that word cards can be hole-punched and hung in place;
- Using a small piece of Velcro, magnetic tape, or sticky tack on both the chart and the word cards; or
- Creating a transparent pocket out of a piece of acetate taped over the word(s) to be substituted.

Shared Reading with a Poem of the Week

Using short poems for shared reading affords many of the same learning opportunities as Big Books, with the added advantage of the "Three Rs": rhythm, rhyme, and repetition. Here is a weekly routine that moves from overall comprehension of the whole text to focusing on its constituent parts: phrases, words, and letters. At the end of the week, the children get their own copies of the poem to keep in their book boxes.

DAY ONE: THE WHOLE POEM

Introduce the poem. Read it aloud, fluently and expressively. Talk with the students about what the poem means. Invite personal connections, wonderings, and aesthetic responses. Reread the poem, inviting students to echo after each line.

DAY TWO: MATCHING LINES OF TEXT

Read the whole poem again, inviting students to join in and fading your own voice out as students' voices get stronger. Have boys and girls take turns reading. Invite students to identify lines of text.

Reproduce lines of text on sentence strips. Have students match the sentence strips to the lines in the poem. Play "mix and fix," by scrambling the lines so students can reassemble them.

DAY THREE: WORKING WITH THE WORDS

Read the poem again, with students taking turns leading the tracking. Let the student leading choose the tracking tool. Engage students in a variety of activities focusing on individual words in the poem, such as:

- naming words for students to "frame" with cupped hands;
- identifying groups, such as rhyming words, action words, plural words, or words that mean the same or opposite;
- "harvesting" high-frequency words for the weekly word wall study;
- teaching two to three unique vocabulary words;
- covering some of the words with blank cards or sticky notes so students can guess the words and uncovering one letter at a time to support their predictions;
- writing silly words on sticky notes and substituting them for words in the text so that students can identify and replace the incorrect words.

DAY FOUR: WORKING WITH LETTERS AND SOUNDS

Read the poem again, perhaps in "silly voices" to keep engagement high. Choose letter features to highlight, such as "twin" letters, silent letters, vowels, or letter patterns. Have students use highlighting tape, or waxy string to identify these letters. Or, make lists of words from the text and sort them (e.g., by meaning, syllables, beginning or ending sounds, or vowel sounds). Have students brainstorm other words that go with words or patterns from the poem.

DAY FIVE: ON YOUR OWN

Give students their own copies of the poem for their individual poetry books. You might have them highlight specific words or text features. Invite students to illustrate their poems and add them to their book boxes for independent reading or take them home to read to their families.

Participating in shared reading activities can have a powerful impact on children's literacy development. David Dickinson found that a shared reading program "dramatically increased children's engagement with books and print in particular," helping them construct knowledge about print and develop self-confidence as readers (1989, 229). However, he cautioned that the type of text, pace of lessons, and focus on textual features inherent in a shared reading experience usually create limited opportunities for extended dialogue about the story and do little to develop higher-level thinking (Dickinson & Smith, 1994). Therefore, it is important that the shared-book experience be just one part of an overall, balanced literacy program that provides many opportunities for reading by, with, and to students.

Check out *Guiding Readers: Making the Most of the 18-Minute Guided Reading Lesson* by Lori Jamison Rog for more information and lesson ideas for small group guided reading.

Small Group Guided Reading

Guided Reading is the next step in increasing student independence as readers. While shared reading tends to be multilevel for large groups, guided reading is targeted to small, needs-based groups. Rather than one enlarged text for all to see, each child has his or her own copy of the text. Texts are carefully selected to support and stretch the students as readers, with teacher-scaffolding as needed.

In today's world of full-day Kindergarten, there is more space in the curriculum for a balance of large group, small group, and individual instruction, along with higher expectations for literacy development before the first grade. However, the research on guided reading in Kindergarten remains sparse, and the practice varies. Some jurisdictions begin small group reading instruction early in the school year while others wait until mid-year, allowing time to build foundational skills and classroom routines. In many cases, it is left to the teacher's professional judgment to determine each student's "readiness" for small group reading instruction. What we do know, however, is that we don't need to wait until students have mastered letter–sound relationships before we put a book in their hands. We know that the sooner they are provided with appropriate materials and appropriate teaching, the more likely they are to make gains in reading (NICHD, 2000).

What does small group guided reading look like in Kindergarten? It might look like a group of students reading and retelling a story together. Or it might look like a teacher and several students playing games with alphabet letters or high-frequency words. Whether we call this instruction "guided reading" or "skills instruction" or simply "reading groups," it serves the same purpose: to provide targeted support for a particular group of students as they build the strategies they need to progress to higher levels.

When we work with small groups, we are better able to identify students' strengths and needs and to provide "just-in-time" teaching to meet those needs. Certainly, by the end of the year (if not the beginning), most of our Kindergarten children will be reading books with a storyline, two or more characters, and several lines of print on the page. We are doing our students a disservice if we fail to provide opportunities for all of them to grow as readers. Small group reading instruction, or guided reading, is one tool for providing those opportunities—as long as we accept that "guided reading" does not look quite the same for emergent readers as it does for any other stage of literacy development.

> **Guided reading with needs-based groups is only one type of grouping structure. Students also need opportunities to participate in interest-based, self-selected, and random groupings.**

Organization and Management: What Are the Other Kids Doing?

It's unrealistic to expect to get a small group reading program up and running at full speed in the first few weeks of school in *any* grade, much less Kindergarten. We can't start working with small groups until the rest of the students can work productively and independently. And let's face it, building the stamina to work productively and independently is an important educational goal in itself. It's probably going to take at least the first six to eight weeks of the school year.

Any independent activity is appropriate for small group reading instruction, as long as it is focused on student learning. In today's play-based classroom, the teacher often pulls small groups while the others are engaged in their own inquiries and explorations. Learning centres have long been a popular structure for independent learning in Kindergarten classrooms and beyond. Some teachers prefer (or are required by their districts) to engage all students in literacy-based activity during certain times of the day. Whether these literacy centre activities involve reading environmental print, building words, or writing letters to classmates, the centres should be targeted toward practicing and extending the strategies students have learned in small group instruction.

> "Guided reading is a sacred time in our classroom. The kids learn quickly that it's a special time, in which interruption means they are stealing the group's learning. Every part of our morning is routine and the kids enjoy the predictability of it."
>
> *Lindsay McGregor, Kindergarten teacher*

One disadvantage of learning centres is that they can be labor-intensive for teachers. Any activity that takes more time for a teacher to prepare than it does for students to complete is a questionable use of time for both! That's why more and more teachers are opting for learning *routines* rather than *activities*. What's the difference? Routines are habits of mind that are self-directed and self-monitored, as opposed to teacher-created, isolated activities. Literacy routines are usually based on reading and writing, such as independent reading, buddy reading, or free choice writing. The advantage is that routines don't require regular preparation or intervention on the part of the teacher and, most importantly, lend themselves to meeting individual needs.

Have a timer on hand to ensure that small group time is kept brief and focused.

Whatever structures we use for independent learning, it's important to model, demonstrate, and practice them before expecting students to engage in them independently. Once the behaviors have been taught, students then practice, starting with brief, timed periods (even just one minute, at first), and gradually increase their stamina to the 15 to 20 minutes needed for a small group reading session. It may take several months to get everyone working independently for 20 minutes, but there is no point in starting any kind of small group instruction until we have this independence in place. Not to mention the fact that when teachers don't have to plan activities to keep "the rest of them" occupied during guided reading, we can dedicate our limited planning time to what matters most—teaching.

When we are confident that all our students can function productively and independently for 20 minutes, we can begin to use that time for assessment and small group instruction. Fifteen to twenty minutes seems optimal for small group time instruction—and long enough to expect independence from the other students.

Twenty minutes of uninterrupted, engaged, self-monitored learning in Kindergarten? It may sound like the impossible dream, but it is not only possible, it is happening in Kindergarten classrooms everywhere.

> Guided reading is a sacred time in our classroom. The kids learn quickly that it's a special time in which interruption means they are stealing learning time from the other students. During literacy time, we never select for the kids which activity they are working on, except for guided reading/small group literacy. We spend a lot of time getting to know the kids and providing activities that will move the kids forward. Activities might include reading (independently or with a partner), writing, retelling familiar stories with story prop boxes, dramatizing, and word games. Since we feel all these activities are valuable, we don't focus too much on which activities kids are going to. Instead, we often help them learn to self-regulate this time of the day by talking about growing our brains and picking things that are challenging. All the kids are engaged, happy, productive, and feeling successful during this time. We've always set out high expectations and the kids routinely strive to meet them.
>
> – *Lindsay McGregor, K/1 teacher*

It's usually a good idea in Kindergarten to schedule an activity break between group times. If the children have been doing sedentary work for 20 minutes, it's time to play a game, sing a song, or simply "shake our sillies out" before returning to independent work. Sometimes we might be able to see two or three groups in a day, but the reality is that we are not going to be able to see every group every day.

We will ensure, however, that every child experiences a rich program of read-aloud, shared reading, writing, and other literacy experiences every day.

Assessment and Grouping

While the students are building stamina as independent learners, we can begin to assess their knowledge of the alphabet, their phonological awareness, and their basic understanding of concepts about print. A running record isn't too useful for students who are not yet reading, but we can conduct many other informal assessments. Hand a student a book backward or upside-down and see if she turns it right-side up before reading. Ask the child if he can distinguish the picture from the words and, if so, whether he can name any letters or words. Identification of alphabet letters, name writing, and hearing sounds in words are other assessments that will help us establish those initial groupings of students with similar instructional needs. As the year goes on and the children begin reading conventionally, we will be able to introduce oral reading records and miscue analysis to our repertoire of assessment tools.

While groups of four to six seem to be optimal for the Kindergarten level, our classes rarely fall so neatly into groups. It may be necessary to split up groups that are too large or combine groups to keep the instruction manageable. You need to decide how many groups will work for you, your students, and your classroom situation: too few, and the group will be too large for individual attention; too many, and you will not be able to see them as often as needed.

The key is keeping groups fluid and flexible. How convenient it would be if all our students progressed at the same rate in the same way! In the real world, we need to constantly assess and adjust our groups to ensure that all students are receiving support that best meets their needs.

Matching Texts and Readers

Guided reading has readers standing on their tiptoes, with the teacher there to balance them as needed.

An important step in planning a guided reading lesson is to find a text that will provide just the right balance of challenge and support for the readers in the group. Ideally, we want the text to be easy enough for the students to tackle most of it on their own, but offer just enough challenge that they will need to draw on reading strategies. The accepted guideline for "instructional" level is that the students will be able to read roughly nine out of ten words in the text and have a general, if not deep, understanding of the material (Betts, 1946). In other words, think of 90 percent support and 10 percent challenge. However, these criteria don't apply to children who are not yet navigating print. Instead, we choose a highly predictable text that they will be able to "read" from pictures and memory.

Leveled texts are a convenience to make text selection easier for teachers. There are many different leveling systems, but all are based on analyzing print features, vocabulary, predictability, and illustrations in the text. The whole point of using leveled texts is to incrementally increase the level—and challenge—for readers. Let's remember, however, that books are leveled, not children! That's why it's important for teachers to understand the leveling criteria; we just can't rely on publishers to make that match for us. It's also important to remember that "instructional level" is for instruction. We never want to limit students to reading only books at "their level."

The Guided Reading Lesson

The guided reading lesson represents a fine balance between careful planning and seizing the "teachable moment." Good teaching should always begin with the end in mind: what do we want these students to take away from this lesson? A lesson may focus on one or more specific comprehension or word-solving behaviors, or on integrating a range of comprehension and word-solving strategies to navigate a text. Once we've decided on the lesson goals, we need to choose a text that will be at an appropriate level of difficulty for this group and that lends itself to those goals. Frontloading the lesson planning will help to make the most of that precious time. Select appropriate pause points in the text, and generate discussion prompts and learning activities during and after group time. There is compelling research supporting the importance of rereading; we usually plan for at least two and often three days with the same text.

Introducing the book forms the bridge between the reader and the text. When planning a book introduction, consider:
- **Preview**
- **Prior knowledge**
- **Purpose**

Before Reading The book introduction may very well be the teacher's most important task in the guided reading sequence. A strong book introduction should provide just enough support to prime the pump, enabling the children to tackle the text and apply their strategies with a degree of independence. As with the read-aloud lesson, the guided reading introduction applies the three P's: preview, prior knowledge, and purpose for reading. To preview the text, introduce the title and author, provide a one-sentence overview of what the book is about, and picture walk some or all the pages in the book. A "pic flic" is a page-by-page preview of the illustrations in the book, intended to get an overview of what the book is about. Activate prior knowledge by inviting students to think about what they already know about the topic or story so they can anticipate what the story will be about and make connections as they read. Sometimes it might be necessary to do some pre-teaching (another P) of vocabulary and concepts, especially for nonfiction reading. Finally, we articulate the purpose for the reading: what do we hope to learn or find out, what strategies are we going to use, and what we should look for in the text.

During Reading During reading, students are usually reading on their own, not in unison nor taking turns round-robin style. That's why it's important that every child has his or her own copy of the text. This process is made more challenging by the fact that most Kindergarten children can't read silently! Some teachers provide "reading phones" made of an elbow of PVC pipe to help keep voices quiet. Another option is to stagger-start the reading so the students aren't all reading the same page at the same time. Remind the students that when they come to the end of the book, they should flip right back to the front and read it again. In fact, it sometimes helps to encourage them to "see how many times you can read this book before I tell you to stop!" While the children are reading, we listen in on each student for a brief few moments, quickly assessing their reading and providing on-the-spot support as needed.

After Reading After reading, we extend children's strategies and experience with the text by talking about what was read, retelling the story, and revisiting the text to focus on individual words, letters, and sounds. Beginning level texts don't usually have much metacognitive meat to chew on, but we can reflect on the various word-solving actions students might have used to access unfamiliar words. If the text lends itself to extended or inferential thinking, prompt the students to explain their ideas or refer to the text to support their thinking. Often we will conclude the reading with a shared or interactive writing lesson, in an effort to make that all-important reading–writing connection.

Generally, the 15-to-20-minute time frame is over long before we have completed this lesson sequence, and the work continues with the same text during the next session. We always spend at least two days with any one book, and often more, depending on the richness of the text.

A Guided Reading Routine for Emergent Readers

Most of our Kindergarten students are likely to be "emergent" readers, at least at the beginning of the year. They may know a lot of things about books and stories and may even pretend to read, but they are not yet connecting letters and sounds. Some teachers believe that students at this stage are not ready for guided reading; however, we believe that putting books in children's hands with appropriate support, even before conventional reading begins, is the very best way to accelerate reading proficiency.

GUIDED READING ROUTINE FOR EMERGENT READERS

1. Teacher reads the text aloud
2. Echo read
3. Choral read
4. Individual read
5. Revisit text to focus on letters, sounds, and words

At this stage, the guided reading lesson is a lot like a modified shared reading lesson, just using little books rather than enlarged print. Because these learners read from pictures and memory, texts at this stage must be highly predictable and patterned, with strong picture support. At the lowest levels, there is only one word on each page, usually labeling the illustration. As the texts increase in difficulty, there may be phrases or even entire sentences on each page, and the pattern might change on the last page of the book. Soon, readers will be expected to sweep their eyes from the end of one line to the beginning of the next, as two lines begin to appear on the page, though these lines are still heavily patterned.

At higher levels, we don't read the whole text aloud for the students, because they are expected to access the print on their own. But it's the only way for emergent readers to make that initial acquaintance with what the text says. We start with a three Ps Introduction (Preview, Prior Knowledge, Purpose for Reading) and a picture walk through the entire book. In this way, we can make sure that there are no unfamiliar words in the text. Then, holding the book up for the students to see and tracking each word, we read each page expressively and fluently (something of a challenge when there are only one or two words on the page).

At this point, the books are distributed so that each student has his or her own copy from which to read. Providing each child with a book in his hands is an important part of guided reading. Lori often provides the students with "reading fingers" ("witch fingers" are available from any dollar store at Halloween). The students and teacher read the text chorally, tracking each word and turning the pages together. After the text has been read several times (and the students have essentially memorized the words), they can go back and "read" it themselves—over and over again. Finally, we revisit this memorized text to match words, isolate letters, look for patterns, and reinforce voice-print matching. That's where the reading manipulatives come in. Giving students trackers (anything with a point, such as chopsticks or stir sticks) and framers (anything with a hole, such as a magnifying glass or a ring) turns word work into play.

In addition to negotiating connected text, guided reading enables students to work with sounds, letters, and words. As much as possible, we use the letters and words in the book as the context for phonemic awareness and phonics practice. Some of the areas of skills focus are defined below:

Phonemic awareness activities for emergent readers might include:

- Clap the syllables in words from the text
- Generate rhymes for words from the text
- Think of words that begin/end with the same sound as key words from the text
- Blend and segment words from the text
- Manipulate words by changing beginning, ending, or medial sounds (sat to cat or sack or sit)
- Use Elkonin boxes or train cars to represent beginning, middle, and ending sounds in words

Name activities for emergent readers might include:

- Provide each student with a bag containing the letters in his/her own name to sort or compare.
- Have students "mix and fix" their own name.
- Play "In my name/not in my name." Name or draw a letter and students must indicate if it's in their name.
- Choose a word from the text. Ask students to compare it with the letters in their own name.

Letter identification activities for emergent readers might include:

- Be detectives and hunt for specific letters in the text.
- Provide each student with an alphabet placemat. Students track and read the letters in different ways: taking turns, with funny voices, just the red letters or the blue letters, etc.
- Play games, like drawing plastic letters out of a bag and naming them. Play "hot potato letters" by naming the letter as quickly as possible and dropping it back in the bag or on the table.
- Say a letter and have students point to it or find it in a "letter pile."

The "Must-Do"

To encourage students to reread their guided reading texts, Lori puts a large sticky note in the back of each book and tells them to get an "autograph" from everyone they read that book to.

After each guided reading session, the students add the book to their individual book boxes and complete a "must-do"—an assigned task that extends the students' experience with the text or provides independent practice on a skill or strategy focused in the lesson.

The "must-do" might involve word hunts, games, word sorts, picture-writing tasks, or reading with a buddy. The whole point of the guided reading lesson is for students to transfer what they have learned to their own independent reading. "Must-Do" activities for emergent readers are always connected to the lesson focus and might include:

- making your own book using the pattern from the text;
- reading the book with a buddy, taking turns reading each page;
- reassembling a copy of the book that's been taken apart;
- matching sentence strips to the print in the book;
- sorting a set of pictures for the letter or sound focus of the lesson;

- working with a partner to sort alphabet letters by letters in each name, letters in both names, letters in neither name;
- playing a game with identifying letters and sounds.

Guided Reading for Early Readers

Once students can write their own names, have a pretty solid mastery of concepts about print, and can apply letter–sound relationships, we consider them to be *early* readers.

Because these readers are connecting letters and sounds, they are starting to be able to navigate print on their own. This is why early-level texts no longer need to be heavily patterned. These texts tend to have more natural language, and illustrations that support the ideas more than the vocabulary. There is often dialogue between two characters. New vocabulary is usually reinforced several times in the text. Because we want to encourage readers at this stage to read in phrases rather than word by word, line breaks in the text occur at meaningful phrases rather than at the end of the space. Here is an opportunity to put away the "reading fingers" and replace them with "sliders" (such as short rulers) to slide under each line.

At this point, we want students to negotiate the guided reading text themselves. We don't read the text aloud to them or invite them to read in chorus. However, we still introduce the book carefully before reading. We might take the students on a picture walk of some or all the illustrations, or invite them to do their own picture walk and "talk to your brain about what you see in the pictures." If some of the vocabulary presents a challenge, we might pre-teach critical words by "building" them with magnetic letters or making connections to known words.

After the book introduction, we hand out the books to the students for them to read independently. As the students read, we listen to each one for a few moments and provide scaffolding and support for miscues. Here's the challenge: Be sure to allow students time for self-corrections! All too often, we teachers intervene before the students even get the words out of their mouths. Count for at least three seconds—or until the reader gets to the end of the page, to give time to realize a word was incorrect. If the child doesn't self-correct, guide her by asking questions like these:

- *Does that word make sense?* If not, invite students to use their other cueing systems to help them read a word that makes sense. Remind students that making sense is the most important part of reading.
- *Does that word sound right?* If the word doesn't sound right in oral language, that's a sign that it's not the right word.
- *Does that word look right?* The final cue is to look at whether the word matches the print. Is that the right beginning or ending sound?

After the reading, revisit the word-solving strategies that the students used during reading. Invite students to retell the story or information. Invite the students to respond by asking, "What do you think about the book?" or prompt them with a "big idea" question.

The second day with the text always begins with an independent rereading. Sometimes, we might take a quick running record, or simply listen to each stu-

Vocabulary: To pre-teach or not to pre-teach?

Is the word critical to understanding a key point in the text? We don't want to take a chance on children missing the word.

Should the children be able to word-solve the word on their own? If it's not decodable or otherwise easy to figure out, we'd better pre-teach it.

Is the word interesting but not essential to the reading? Give the children a chance to solve it on their own and revisit it after reading to talk about strategies a reader might use.

dent read and offer support as needed. We might play a quick game to reinforce high-frequency words or key vocabulary from the text. As with emergent readers, we revisit the text to focus on letters, words, and patterns as needed by the students. Highlight high-frequency words, look at word families, and build words. Spend the last five minutes of the lesson on a guided writing task, such as a dictated or open-ended sentence. Additional small group activities for early readers may be found below.

<table>
<tr>
<td valign="top">

Word-solving activities for early readers

- Mix and fix with magnetic letters or letter tiles
- Word and letter hunts in the text
- Build "ladders" of rhyming words
- Karate chop the word into parts
- "Read my mind" (Students guess a hidden word, as one letter at a time is revealed)
- Vowel-sound Bingo
- Read around the word (context clues)
- Look for parts you know

</td>
<td valign="top">

Comprehension activities for early readers

- Retelling
- "Talking to your brain" (Self-talk during reading)
- Self-monitoring (semantic, syntactic, phonetic cues)
- Talking about "I wonder" and "I think"

</td>
<td valign="top">

Fluency activities for early readers

- Moving a slider under each line of text to read in phrases
- Talking like the talker (expression in dialogue)
- Pausing at the period

</td>
</tr>
</table>

Following the lesson, "must-do" activities might include:

- Writing around the room: Students tour the room with a clipboard, writing any words they find that meet specific criteria related to the word work from the story, such as words ending in /s/ or words with double letters.
- High-frequency words: Reinforce high-frequency words from the story. Provide letter stamps or magnetic letters for the students to read each word, build it, then write it on paper or a magnetic white board.
- Copycat stories: Children write their own stories.
- Reading some more: Provide a book on a similar topic or by the same author, at a slightly easier reading level.

Never before has differentiating reading instruction been more important. We are dealing with increasing ranges of skill and ability, varying amounts of oral-language development, and huge differences in the amount of literacy experiences our Kindergarten children bring to school with them. Some children arrive at our door already knowing how to navigate print and make meaning from books. Others might simply have had limited opportunities to interact with books or even build English-language skills. We have always known that one size doesn't fit all in reading instruction. Guided reading, as one part of a balanced literacy program, helps us fit every student.

6

Learning to Write and Writing to Learn

Everyone knows that reading makes us smarter. But did you also know that *writing* makes us smarter? Writing helps us organize our ideas and put them into words. Janet Emig (1977) was one of the first researchers to pay attention to the value of writing to learn. She reported that because writing requires active engagement with information, it helps learners understand and retain information better. Writing to learn requires learners to process what they already know, enabling them to stretch their thinking and opens their minds to new ideas.

In the famous "90-90-90 Schools" study, Doug Reeves (2000) and his colleagues looked at schools with 90 percent of the students in poverty, 90 percent of the students having minority backgrounds, and 90 percent of the students scoring at or above grade level on independent performance assessments; in other words, schools that were beating the odds. Among the common practices of these schools, from Kindergarten to college, was writing in every subject area, all day long.

There are many things we can do to create the conditions for a Kindergarten classroom in which writing to learn is practiced and valued. Here are just some of them:

Labeling Constructions and Creations: There are many benefits to having students name the things they create, whether the creations are produced from blocks or paint or found materials. It tells others what they have accomplished. It helps them remember what they made and what they learned long after the blocks have been turned into something else. And it builds ownership in both the process and the product. Some teachers provide time at the end of each day for children to share their learning; having a written record can help some children remember just what it was they created earlier that morning.

Wonder Walls and Discovery Centres: Many classrooms have charts on hand for students to record questions they're wondering about. (These are excellent tools for further inquiry.) Why not divide the paper in half for students to suggest answers to the questions posed, perhaps distinguishing the "I think" answers from the "I know" answers. At discovery centres, invite students to write "I see/I think" responses.

Inquiry Research: Any time children are conducting research on a question or problem, they should be given opportunities to document what they learn. They take notes (in pictures or words) to remember facts and create projects to celebrate their learning.

Recording Special Events: Create class books for children to write and draw about important events in their lives, such as the "Lost and Loose Tooth Book." Writing in the "Ouch Book" can sometimes ease the pain of an injury. (Provide a package of Band-Aids for students to add to their illustrations.) A "Classroom Concerns" bag in which children can record suggestions or questions might just be the solution for those who whine or tattle. Instruct children to write down their problems and put them in the bag for the teacher to look at later.

Writing about Reading: Create a place near the book nook where students can write or draw about books they've read or even make book recommendations for others.

Daily Sign-in: The National Early Literacy Panel (2009) identified the ability to recognize and write one's own name as an essential pre-literacy competency. Have children "sign in" for attendance each day to practice writing their names. After they learn their first names, invite children to write their surnames as well. Later in the year, sign-in time can take the form of a survey in which children write their names beside favorite foods or colors. Ultimately, they may even sign in with whole sentences, such as "What I Like to Do After School."

"How-to" Writing: How to clean up the construction zone. What to feed the pet hamster. How to help a friend read. The authentic opportunities for procedural writing in Kindergarten are unlimited.

Weekend Journals: Each week, have the children document their learning or classroom experiences to take home and share with their families.

Not all our Kindergarten students will be at the same stage of readiness to write at the same time. They might be drawing, adding scribbles, copying print from around the room, or even using invented spelling. Only the teacher knows when to nudge, when to support, and when to celebrate just where they are. But our children can't use writing to learn effectively unless they have opportunities for learning to write. That's where explicit instruction comes in.

Several years ago, researcher Donald Graves (1983) asked a group of kindergartners whether they knew how to read. Only a handful responded that they could read. Then he asked the same children how many knew how to write. Almost all of them raised their hands! This is not surprising. For many of our children, writing develops more easily and naturally than reading. As soon as they know that pictures tell a story, they're starting to recognize that they can communicate messages with a pen or crayon. So, how can we help them move from pictures and scribbles to using letters and sounds in ways that others can read? If we want our students to become increasingly confident and competent writers, we need to show them what writers do.

Modeling may very well be the most important tool in our instructional toolboxes. We model writing for students not only to demonstrate how writers think and work, but also to show students that writing is an important and meaningful activity that people do in life as well as in school. When we think aloud as we write, we are giving our beginning writers a glimpse of the "in the head" processes that writers go through as they transfer an idea in their minds to symbols on a page.

Modeling and demonstrating the mechanics and processes of writing involves teacher–student interactions at varying levels of support and independence, including modeled, shared, interactive, guided, and independent writing.

Showing Students What Writers Do

Showing children what their talk looks like in print has long been an effective practice in Kindergarten. The traditional "language experience approach" still has plenty of merit, but we now recognize that we're missing valuable learning opportunities if we focus only on the product and not on the process of composing and transcribing ideas.

Modeled writing instruction should always begin with a learning goal related to a writing strategy as opposed to a product, such as "write a story about spring." Sometimes we want to bring the whole class together for a message that we want them all to hear, such as introducing a new text form. At other times, we'll work with small groups or individuals on strategies targeted to their specific needs.

There are different forms of modeling, from modeled writing with high teacher involvement and low student interaction to guided writing with high student involvement and minimal teacher support.

Modeled Writing: "Writing Out Loud"

Three Ways to Write in Kindergarten
- **"Curly Writing"** (scribbles)
- **"ABC Writing"** (random letters)
- **"Book Writing"** (conventional spelling)

In a modeled writing experience, the teacher explains what is going on in his mind as he demonstrates what writers do. He shows the students that good writers write by thinking of ideas, talking about their ideas, and putting those ideas on paper using letters and words. In this process, the students are observers, not active participants. For example, Lori often starts the year with a lesson modeling "Three Ways to Write in Kindergarten." She introduces a topic such as "What I did on my summer holidays" and a detail, such as "I went camping in the mountains." Explaining that in Kindergarten we use pictures and writing to tell stories, just like in the books we read, Lori starts by drawing a quick sketch of herself in her tent in the mountains. Then she models how to write the words: in "curly" (scribble) writing, in "ABC" (random letters or invented spelling) writing, and in "book" (conventional) writing. Together, they practice all three forms of writing before the students are expected to write on their own using one or more of the three forms. When introducing "book writing," Lori models writing the word "I"—*a word that you will need in almost everything you write. So, when you hear your voice say 'I', it should look like this: a straight line down and little lines across the top and the bottom.* Modeled writing is an opportunity for the teacher to provide brief but explicit instruction.

Shared Writing: Seeing Our Talk Written Down

We've just come back from a field trip to the local museum and we want the students to compose a collaborative report on the highlights of the excursion. We might get out a sheet of chart paper or fire up the interactive whiteboard and invite the students to contribute ideas, while the teacher does the actual writing.

This is called "shared writing." The students are partners in determining the *what*; the teacher scribes to demonstrate the *how*.

Language experience activities such as this enable children to see their talk written down. Together, the teacher and students negotiate what will be written. This is a powerful oral-language activity, as children learn to string ideas together in coherent words and sentences. Using some form of enlarged print, the teacher writes the words that students compose, modeling and demonstrating the process of putting those ideas in print. We often call the products of this activity "experience charts," though in today's Kindergarten classroom, they are completed on an interactive whiteboard as often as on a large piece of paper. These actual or virtual charts are revisited frequently as shared and independent reading texts.

Interactive Charts

Instead of having the group collaborate on a composition, record one idea from each student. This process is often done individually or in small groups, rather than with the whole class. (It will be neither interesting nor educational for students to sit through the transcription of every student response in the class.) Here is a one-on-one opportunity for differentiating the language experience for each student.

Print by hand or word-process the students' responses on a large chart, which may be revisited several times for students to "read" their own responses and those of others. When the chart has served its purpose as a shared reading and language instruction tool, cut apart the individual student responses into strips. Glue each student's sentence strip onto a piece of paper and invite that student to read and illustrate it. Digital cameras make it easy to provide each student with a photograph of himself or herself to incorporate into the illustration. Depending on the developmental level of the students, you may choose to cut apart the individual words and have the student reassemble them and glue them down on the page. The illustrated pages may then be stapled or coiled together in a book for the classroom library or take-home reading program.

Interactive Writing: Sharing the Pen

In an interactive writing lesson, the teacher and students collaborate on both the composing and the writing. Heavily scaffolded by the teacher, individual students take turns "sharing the pen" to write the message. The teacher selects individual students to do the writing. Depending on their stage of readiness, some students might be invited to write just a few letters, while other students will be able to write some sight words. There is much research to support interactive writing as a powerful means of supporting understanding of syntax, phonemic awareness, phonics, sentence structure, grammar, and punctuation (Jones, et al., 2010).

Interactive writing tends to be slow and methodical. Only one or two students are actively involved at any given time; for this reason, interactive writing is most effective with individuals or small groups. But even with a small group of students, it's important to engage the other students in the group by inviting them to share in the composition of ideas and to think about letters, patterns, and words.

Tip for reinforcing word boundaries
Have one student serve as the "writer" and another act as the "spacer" who puts his or her hand after each word to mark the space before the next word is written.

What are the other kids doing?
Kids who aren't doing the actual
writing might be invited to:

- Count on their fingers the
  number of words in the message
- Put on their "magic glasses"
  (fingers around their eyes) and
  look for high-frequency words in
  the room
- Trace words and letters on the
  floor or on a partner's back
- Practice writing words or letters
  on individual white boards

We might only get a sentence or two on the page in a day's lesson. The students learn that sometimes we have to go back on another day to read what we've written and add more details. It is a good lesson for students to see a writing project extend over a few days.

Even in a brief lesson, we can reinforce many concepts about language and print, from distinguishing uppercase and lowercase letters to using the word wall to help spell words. And, as we write, we go back over and over again to read what we've written. Here, we are reminding students of an amazing feature of writing: that it says the same thing every time we read it.

Guided Writing: Your Turn

In guided writing, the students are doing the writing, but with lots of teacher support. Often, we use guided writing for children to practice a strategy that has been modeled before we expect them to use it on their own. For example, after Lori models "Three Ways to Write in Kindergarten" (page 71), she has the students practice each of the writing forms on their individual whiteboards. Rather than focusing on a writing product, the guided writing exercise focuses on a strategy or element of process. As always, the teacher's assessment of student needs is the best guide for planning guided writing instruction.

Shared, interactive, and guided writing are the "We Do" of the gradual release of responsibility. Children who receive this balance of challenge and support are not only more motivated to write, they are more willing to experiment and take risks in their writing. As one kindergartner was heard to exclaim, "I never knew I could write this good!"

Independent Writing: The Writing Workshop

Generally, the Kindergarten
writing workshop lasts about 30-40
minutes:
Teaching time: 5-10 minutes
Writing time: about 20 minutes
Sharing time: 5-10 minutes

Modeling and guided practice are important structures for teaching students what writers do. But children also need many opportunities to write on their own, while being supported, nudged, and scaffolded to higher levels. That's where the writing workshop comes in. There are many variations to the writing workshop structure, but it generally consists of three components: some teaching time, some writing time, and some sharing time. This is the time for students to practice the strategies and processes they have been taught. The great strength of the writing workshop, however, is the independence it fosters. Children are taught from the outset that it is their responsibility to choose topics, to solve their own problems, and to keep working until writing time is over.

The teaching part of the writing workshop consists of a short period of explicit teaching and guided practice that addresses a specific learning goal. The challenge for teachers is to keep this instruction brief and focused; that's why we call it a *minilesson*. Ten minutes should be long enough to model a strategy without losing the students' attention. Sometimes it might even be necessary to set a timer for ten minutes; when the timer sounds, the lesson stops, to be continued another day. Within that ten minutes we try to model and think-aloud a specific strategy (I Do), and then give the students a chance to practice it, usually in a shared writing context (We Do). During writing time, students are expected to incorporate the strategy into their own writing (You Do).

Writing time is the longest and most important part of the writing workshop. At first, many of our students will not have the stamina to work on their own for very long, but gradually their attention span will increase to 20 minutes and sometimes more. In writing workshop, students are required to use their writing time responsibly. This means that when they finish one task, they move on to another—without teacher intervention. We teach our Kindergarten writers that they can always add more details to their picture, add more writing, or start a new piece. No one should ever have to ask, "What do I do when I'm done?" because "When you're done, you've just begun!" This routine takes a lot of modeling and practice, but it's well worth the time, both to build student self-regulation and to free the teacher up to provide individual and small group support.

Teaching Emergent Writers

When they first arrive at the door of Kindergarten, most of our children are "emergent" readers and writers. This means that they are not yet connecting letters and sounds to decode and to spell. Donna-Lynn introduces the writing workshop to her students with an analogy about learning to talk. She tells the students that when they were babies, they could only cry and their moms and dads had to figure out that they were hungry. Gradually, they learned to say words like "wawa" and some other people, like grandpa and grandma, knew what they wanted. Now that they're in Kindergarten, they can say, "Please, may I have a glass of water?" and everyone knows what they mean. Writing is a little bit like that. At first, they might be the only ones who know what their writing says but, gradually, they learn to use more letters and words and other people can read what they say.

Most of us have been trained to think of "the writing process" as five steps: planning, drafting, revising, editing, and publishing. But kindergartners rarely "publish" their work and it serves no pedagogical purpose to have five-year-old children correct and recopy their writing. For most beginning writers, pre-writing is actually pre-telling; they start by telling a partner what they're going to write about. Then they write by drawing a picture and adding some "writing" (see "Three Ways to Write in Kindergarten" on page 71). They complete the process by writing their name and using a date stamp to record the date.

Writing workshop is simple! The only equipment needed is something to write on and something to write with. We advocate providing unlined paper for kindergartners; we want them to be able to experiment with placing pictures and letters on the page. And they write with markers, not pencils. We don't want them spending all of writing time erasing. So, we teach them to "strikethrough" words and letters they want to delete or replace. It's sometimes hard for children to understand that it's okay to make mistakes and it's okay to change your mind as you write, but that's what writers do.

While the students are writing, the teacher is buzzing around the room, visiting each student individually to ask what their writing says or what's happening in their pictures, and to offer advice to move the writer along. The teacher might ask a question like, "What games do you like to play with your dog?" and suggest that the student add the appropriate detail to the picture and/or the writing. Or the teacher might focus on conventions, such as, "Your dog's name is Oliver. That starts just the same as Opreet on our name wall. Please put an 'O' right there for Oliver."

Sharing time is an important way to end the writing workshop. Each day, two or three children can read-aloud a piece of writing of their choice (sometimes with the teacher's help). It is both a privilege and a responsibility to share writing. The other students provide stars (compliments) and wishes (questions).

Invented Spelling (a.k.a. Bubble Gum Writing)

Bubble Gum Writing, Sticky Dot Details, and many other tools are described more fully in Lori's book *Marvelous Minilessons for Teaching Nonfiction Writing K–3* (Pembroke, 2015).

Since most children are not yet connecting letters and sounds, alphabet work and the phonetic principle are key areas of focus at this stage. Invented or temporary spelling is one of the most powerful tools we have for reinforcing phonemic awareness and phonics in context. And research has shown that children who are encouraged to spell phonetically actually become better conventional spellers down the road because they've learned to experiment with the ways that language goes together. Lori calls phonetic spelling "Bubble Gum Writing." She tells the children to pretend a word is a piece of bubble gum in their mouths and s-t-r-e-t-c-h the word out with one hand while using the other hand to write a letter for every sound they hear. As our children learn to put letters together into words and words into sentences, we turn more attention to the craft of writing, such as adding details, using powerful words, and applying different text forms.

Topics and Details: We teach children that writing is made up of *details* that stick to a *topic*. The topic is what the writing is about; each piece of information about the topic is a detail. We always have our students tell others in the group what they're going to write about before putting their ideas on paper. When children share their ideas, it helps them organize their thinking (and often it inspires those who can't think of what to write about). Lori likes to give her students large colorful sticky dots from the dollar store. She tells them to put a "dot" at the end of each detail. This can be a very motivating means of getting students over the "one-detail" hurdle.

It takes a lot of effort for our Kindergarten children to decide what to write about, where to draw the picture, what details to add, what writing to use, and how to form those letters on the page. The great thing about writing workshop is that every child can participate at his or her own level. Our children will be at many different stages of writing development and we need to honor every mark on those pages. Some children might need to write in another language before they are comfortable with English; in fact, writing is an excellent entry point into literacy for English language learners and other students with limited oral-language skills. And our job as teachers is to know which students to challenge, which ones to nudge, and which ones to celebrate exactly where they are.

7

Putting the "Play" Back in Word Play

When Lori's grandson first discovered language play, he took great delight in coming up with rhyming names for his grandfather: What do we call Papa when he makes a mess? Sloppa! What do we call him when he cleans it up? Moppa! Games like these can help to instill an interest in and love of language that will support his literacy development for a long time.

The appearance of literacy centres on the day's schedule always elicits cheers from my Kindergarten students. I call it "play with a purpose," but they just call it fun. Literacy centre activities are designed for children to practice and develop the skills and concepts currently under study, possibly the alphabet, sight words, sequencing, or sentence construction, depending on the stage of development or point in the school year. The activities might require a group of students to work co-operatively—for example, to play an alphabet bingo game—or could involve individual parallel play where each child builds words with magnetic letters.

My class is divided into groups composed by the activity or my intended learning goal. The groups could be of mixed or similar academic ability, or a supportive social group, or even entirely random. Before moving to literacy centres, activities and materials are introduced to the whole class, with discussion around appropriate behaviors and handling of materials. Favorite literacy centre activities include writing in shaving cream on tabletops, stacking plastic cups printed with sight words into pyramids, retelling stories using felt shapes or toys as props, making sentences out of colored paper chains, and reading sight words clipped to a friend's clothing.

Ann George, Kindergarten teacher

But, somewhere along the line, "word *play*" disappeared and was replaced by "word *work*." Pressures on children to be conventional readers at earlier ages and pressures on teachers to make that happen have made learning about letters and words serious business. In some Kindergarten classrooms, we're more likely to see children completing worksheets than building with blocks. However, there are many ways to fill our Kindergarten children's literate lives with engaging, interactive, and developmentally appropriate experiences with letters and words that are both playful and purposeful.

Learning the Alphabet

Alphabet knowledge is widely regarded as an important precursor to literacy. Although different jurisdictions vary in their requirements of how many letters children are expected to know by the end of Kindergarten, it remains true that the more they know, the easier reading will be. And our ultimate goal is for *all* of the students to know *all* of the letters, even if not all students will reach that goal.

Rapid automatic naming of alphabet letters and understanding letter-sound relationships were both identified by the National Early Learning Panel (2008) as an essential "preliteracy" skill. Children can learn the sounds of the letters at the same time they learn the letter names. After all, 22 of the 26 letters in the English alphabet have their sounds in their names. The connection between the letters and the sounds they represent is known as the "alphabetic principle." Knowing the relationship between the sounds in words (phonemic awareness) and the symbols on the page (phonics) is an important step in reading development.

Not long ago, learning letter names was a goal of Kindergarten; today, many children know their letters long before they start school. Most children whose first language is English arrive at school knowing something about the written code. But some letters are easier to learn and remember than others. Laura Justice and her colleagues (2006) reported the following findings about letter knowledge:

- The first letters children learn—and that are most solidly remembered—are the letters in their own names.
- Letters at the beginning of the alphabet are mastered slightly more quickly than those at the end; letters in the middle of the alphabet are often the most difficult to recall.
- Letters with their sounds in their names and with consistent letter–sound relationships are more easily retained.
- Letters that appear frequently in familiar words—names of others, names of objects, environmental print—are mastered more quickly.
- Some children learn letters by attending to their distinctive features: lines, curves, circles, and intersections.

What does this tell us about teaching the alphabet? For one thing, different children know and learn different letters at different rates. For another, not all letters merit the same amount of attention. That's why whole class programs that focus on one letter a week from *a* to *z* are not the best use of anyone's time. "Letter of the Week" routines fail to acknowledge the differing needs and background knowledge of the students. Not only that, these routines introduce letters in alphabetical sequence, not in an order that has the most meaning for children. Finally, this routine takes virtually an entire school year just to introduce the letters; and some of the most frequently used letters—*r*, *s*, and *t*, for example—don't appear until the last half of the alphabet.

So, if time-honored traditions and routines don't work, what does? Brief, explicit teaching sessions, repeated exposure and practice, and instruction targeted to the needs of students are what works, according to early childhood expert William Teale (2015).

Cindy Jones and her colleagues at the University of Utah (2012) have come up with a teaching routine they call Enhancing Alphabet Knowledge (EAK). Students are introduced to one letter each day in a brief, ten-minute instructional session that involves introducing the letter names and sounds, identify-

EAK 10-Minute Routine
1. Identify and name the upper and lower case forms of the letter.
2. Identify the main sound the letter represents.
3. Guide students in recognizing the letter in connected text.
4. Point out distinctive visual features and have students practice printing the letter.

ing the letters in print, and producing them in writing. Teaching one letter a day enables the teacher to repeat the alphabet cycle up to six times throughout the year, each time presenting the letters in a different order. These researchers recommend starting the year by introducing the initial letters of the children's (and other significant) names, followed by reviewing all the letters in alphabetical order, through environmental print, and by visual features. After the first cycle, teachers can assess which students know which letters, and they might pull selected groups for instruction during subsequent cycles. For example, the day that focuses on *s* (a letter that appears frequently in words and is distinctive in both shape and sound) might involve a very small group, whereas there might be quite a large group on *n* day, a letter difficult to distinguish from *m* in both appearance and sound. In this way, the letters are introduced quickly, and then reinforced as needed throughout the school year. Once a child has mastered a letter, there's no need to keep reviewing it. Ultimately, we want to teach letters early and quickly, then reinforce them as needed, so that children can actually use the letters in connected reading and writing.

When it comes to intervention, Jeffri Brookfield and colleagues (2013) found that a set of 13 sessions of only two- to four-minutes each was enough to bring most children up to standards. Teachers in British Columbia's School District 59 worked with Professor Janet Mort to develop what they call "the blitz." After an individual needs-assessment, children receive brief, intensive, game-based sessions focused on their specific targets.

We spend an hour once a week "blitzing" students on the word analysis skills they need most. Much of the time, we're focused on sight words or alphabet letters and sounds. Each teacher assesses his or her students individually and forms small groups based on needs. During the hour, children rotate through six or seven stations for about ten minutes each. Ideally there is an adult—teacher, paraprofessional or volunteer—at each station. These stations are quick, interactive, and, most of all, fun! They usually have some kind of word game or playful activity, such as:

- Crash! A game where students read a sight word or name a letter and then roll the dice to move toy cars around a racetrack game board.
- Read It, Write It, Smell It, Hide It: Students draw a word card. If they can read it, they get to write it in smelly markers, smell it, then keep the word in their brains as they "hide it" (flip the paper over) and write the word on the other side of the page.
- Rainbow Write: Each number on the die corresponds to a color. Students go through sight word cards one at a time. For each word, they roll the die and write the word in that color (e.g., 1-purple, 2-blue, 3-green, 4-orange, 5-red, 6-brown).

Throughout the rest of the week, students would continue to work on their target skills as teachers continuously assess their progress and determine the focus for their next "blitz."

Kristy Lineham, Kindergarten teacher

Of course, letter–sound correspondences are best taught within the context of a print-rich literacy environment. High quality read-alouds, purposeful shared reading, targeted small group instruction, interactive writing experiences, and opportunities for meaningful use of the alphabet provide the just-in-time teaching and guided practice that most children need. It's important that instructional decisions be based on assessments of what children already know and what they need to learn next, such as:

- Which upper- and lower-case letters can this student identify, in isolation and in a word?
- Can this student identify/produce the most common sounds related to those letters?
- Can this student distinguish letter-sound sounds at the beginning, end, and middle of a word?
- Can this student print the upper- and lower-case letter?
- Can this student apply knowledge of letter–sound relationships to writing whole words?

The Name Wall

What's the most important word in any child's vocabulary? His or her own name, of course! For most children, their names are the first words they learn to write. Even children who do not have the background experiences or fine motor skills to print their own names can often recognize their names in print. Our children's own names are the most powerful contexts we have for providing systematic instruction in alphabet letters and sounds.

It's easy to create a "Name Wall" in the Kindergarten classroom. You probably already have a space to display the children's names. The wall space should be accessible and visible to all students and include a display of each letter of the alphabet in uppercase and lowercase form. This wall will be used to feature the children's names, one at a time, for word work—and play. The alphabet wall will probably remain in place all year, perhaps to later include high-frequency words.

Each day, appoint a different person to be the leader of the day. The leader's name will be spelled, chanted, cheered, printed, and posted on the name wall that day. The other students might "interview" the leader of the day, a routine that provides important oral-language practice in asking and answering questions. If we record two or three of the responses on a large sheet of paper, the leader can illustrate his or her page and all the pages can later be bound into a class book. Not only does this routine introduce alphabet letters in the context of children's names, it also builds community in the classroom as each child is celebrated and the children get to know one another.

Use the initial letter of each child's name as an introduction to that letter, its sound, and its visual features, then go hunting for that letter in other words around the room. Have children practice printing the featured letter, and the whole name if appropriate. Of course, you will have more than one name beginning with the same letter and some letters that are not represented in your class at all. You might use the name of your school, your town, or the principal of your school to supplement the name wall. Concept words such as "house" for H and "fish" for F are also useful. One resourceful teacher had a menagerie of stuffed animals that she named each year by the letters that were missing in her class.

And let's not forget that the same letter can represent different sounds—consider Jennifer, Jakub, and Juanita—another powerful learning experience.

Teaching time for letter-names is also an excellent opportunity for the children to learn to print the letters. Guide the children to identify the visual features of the letter and what it has in common with other letters.

The final step each day is to add the name to the name wall and compare it with other names on the wall—number of letters, the same letters, syllables, etc.

Daily Name Wall Routine (10 minutes)

1. Pick a name from the name basket. This person becomes the leader for the day.
2. Have students interview the leader by asking questions, such as "How many brothers and sisters do you have?" or "What's your favorite food?"
3. Focus on the initial letter in the child's name. Name the letter and the sound it represents. Look at its visual features: tall letter, tail letter, round letter, straight letter? How will students remember that letter?
4. Look for other words in the room that contain the featured letter.
5 Practice forming the letter, tracing it in the air, on the floor, or on the table, and printing it on paper or on an individual white board.
6. Post the name on the name wall, count the letters and compare it to other names on the wall. Which have more letters? Which have fewer letters? Which have letters that are the same?

The leader chooses how to call the letters of his/her name:
- cheering the letters
- chanting the letters
- singing the letters to a familiar tune
- marching, hopping, or doing another action as the letters are called out

---

There are many benefits to the name wall routine. First, it presents language concepts in the context of meaningful words rather than in isolation. Second, it enables teachers to cover the entire alphabet in just over a month rather than in 26 weeks (as with one letter per week). Once the name wall is on display, we can use it to reinforce and apply letter–sound knowledge. As you draw students' attention to words, point out, "This word starts the same as *Dylan*," or "This word ends like *Sunil*."

The name wall is an excellent tool for systematic introduction and reinforcement of the sounds and structures of letters and words. It is also a good reminder that alphabet letters are tools for reading and writing, and not ends in themselves. The reason we use letters is to write our names and all other words.

The name wall routine generally takes no more than five or ten minutes and is conducted with the whole class. However, there are many other playful activities that reinforce phonics and phonemic awareness through children's names in small groups or independent learning routines, such as:

- preparing sets of name cards for various types of word sorts, such as: numbers of syllables, numbers of letters, names that have the letters in my name, or names of boys and names of girls.

Place mats with the alphabet printed on them can be purchased very economically at your local dollar store. For a reproducible alphabet arc, see www.fcrr.org/Curriculum/pdf/GK-1/Archive/F_Final.pdf

- providing students with sets of alphabet letters or "Scrabble"-type tiles to find letters in their names and not in their names.
- playing games like "Wheel of Fortune," with students trying to figure out a hidden name by guessing one letter at a time, or BINGO with students' names on the bingo card. Have students fill a blank card by printing their own name in the centre square and asking eight friends to print their names in the remaining squares.
- practicing letter formation by tracing letters in well-sealed zipper bags containing shaving cream or hair gel, or doing "rainbow writing" by tracing the letters with at least three different colored markers.
- going on "treasure hunts" for letters in books or environmental print using pointers, framers, or "reading glasses" (old sunglasses with the lenses removed).
- printing sets of letters in various fonts, colors, and sizes, for identifying, comparing, and sorting.

Letter Patterns

Once our children know how to connect letters to the individual sounds they represent, we also want them to begin to identify letter patterns, such as consonant blends, vowel digraphs, and "word families" or rimes. A rime consists of a vowel and the letters that follow it in a syllable, such as "ill" or "ake." The "onset" is the phoneme at the beginning of the rhyme, such as the *b* in *bill* or the *sh* in *shake.* Learning these familiar patterns opens the door to a wealth of words for reading and writing. As well, introducing vowel sounds through rimes is far more consistent than by the traditional "long" and "short" patterns. While consonants represent the same sound pretty much all the time, vowels only represent their traditional "long" or "short" sounds about half the time. However, vowel sounds in rimes are consistent about 75 percent of the time.

Lori's favorite routine for introducing a new rime or word family starts with a "word family house" drawn on a piece of paper, with the focus rime at the top. Together, she and the students brainstorm some words that include that rime. They don't need every possible word; a list of six to eight words is generally enough to reinforce the pattern. The advantage of the house metaphor is that if students suggest a word that has the same sound but a different spelling, as in *crawl,* we can add it to the corner of the page outside the house and say, "It's in the neighborhood, but it's not in the family." These word family house posters become reference points for reading and writing other words that contain those rimes.

Of course, rimes aren't the only letter patterns that are required for reading and writing. Instruction in consonant blends *(tr, bl),* digraphs *(sh, th),* and vowel combinations *(ea, oi)* will also be part of the word study curriculum. The "Making Words" strategy developed by Patricia Cunningham (Cunningham & Allington, 2007) is a systematic approach to word study which guides students to manipulate letters and letter patterns to form words. Starting with a group of letters like *s, n, o,* and *w,* children might be instructed to make *on, no, so, sow, own,* and *now.* Then they're given the challenge of coming up with one word that uses all the letters. An important component of this routine is to sort the words in various ways, then come up with other words that might fit the patterns. For example, students might group *sow* and *now,* then add *wow* and *cow* to the group. This provides an

Over 500 primary words may be generated from the following 37 basic rimes:

ack	aw	ink
ain	ay	ip
ake	eat	it
ale	ell	ock
all	est	oke
ame	ice	old
an	ick	op
ank	ide	ore
ap	ight	ot
ash	ill	uck
at	in	ug
ate	ing	ump
		unk

opportunity to talk about different pronunciations of the *ow* dipthong as well as multiple meanings and pronunciations for words like *sow* or *bow*.

High-Frequency Words

Ninety percent of the reading we do, even as adults, is made up of only 5,000 words (Laberge & Samuels, 1974). No wonder they're called "high frequency"! Of these, the first 25 are mostly conjunctions (*and, so*), prepositions (*on, in, up*), verbs of being (*is, am*), and articles (*the, a*). Whether they're called "snap" words (because we need to be able to read and write them in a snap) or "popcorn" words (because they keep popping up everywhere) or simply "sight" words, these are the words that glue sentences together. That's why readers need to access them automatically for fluent reading and writing. What makes these words particularly difficult is that most of them don't follow regular letter–sound patterns and many defy definition. They just have to be memorized.

It is generally expected that Kindergarten children will develop a small repertoire of these common words, and that by the end of first grade, they will have mastered at least 100 high-frequency words. There are no universal guidelines on exactly how many words kindergartners should have in their sight word repertoires, but, as Donna Scanlon and her colleagues (2011) point out, "Because knowledge of high-frequency words provides children with so much access to reading materials, and allows them to be strategic in learning new words, setting higher expectations for sight word knowledge is probably in the children's best interests" (228).

Ideally, high-frequency words are harvested from shared reading and writing experiences, so children can be exposed to the words both in context and in isolation. We use a range of modes of learning—visual, auditory, and kinesthetic—to reinforce each word. We might become "reading detectives" with magnifying glasses to hunt for the word in connected text, or "read around the room" to find it in environmental print. We spell the word orally, chanting it (often with finger snaps or hand claps), cheering it ("Give me a C!"), and even singing it (such as spelling the word *are* to the tune of "Three Blind Mice"). We do actions, such as "bowling" each letter, cheering the whole word as we get a "strike" at the end, or "striking at" each letter with a pretend bat and getting a "home run" as we say the whole word at the end. Finally, we print the word, tracing it in the air, on the floor, even on a partner's back before putting marks on the page.

In many Kindergarten classrooms, high-frequency words are displayed on a word wall, to be reviewed, reinforced, revisited, and retrieved as a resource for reading and writing. Only two or three words are taught each week, making sure that these words are mastered before adding more. It's also important to teach students consistent routines for "borrowing" words from the word wall, such as the one in "A Simple Word Wall Routine."

Use word walls with caution! Too many words make the walls cluttered and overwhelming. Only post words on the wall that have been taught and reinforced. In fact, when all children have mastered a word, it can be retired from the word wall.

Here are some other playful ways to reinforce high-frequency words:

- ***Shower Curtain Games***: Shower curtain liners from the dollar store offer potential for any number of active games. Use a marker to divide the shower

A Simple Word Wall Routine
1. **Find the word.**
2. **Say the letters to yourself.**
3. **Take a picture of the word in your mind.**
4. **Write the word.**

curtain into large squares and write a high-frequency word on each square. Students may walk, hop, or skip along the squares, reading the words as they step on them, or do a beanbag toss and read the word on which the bean bag lands. Students like to play "musical words," in which they march on the squares to music, with a clipboard in their hands. When the music stops, they must read or write the word they are standing on. It's also possible to create a variation of "Twister," in which players are instructed to put their left foot or their right hand on a given word.

- *Sight Word Tally*: Give students a highlighter and a page from a magazine. Assign two sight words that the students must highlight each time they appear on the page. Invite students to tally how frequently each word appears on the page and determine which word "wins." It doesn't matter that the students can't read the whole text; the point of the exercise is to practice automatic recognition of the high-frequency words.

- *X-Ray Eyes*: Margo Southall (2009) suggests systematically removing letters from a known word and teaching students to "see and say" the missing letters. Write a word and chant the letters with the students. As you erase one letter at a time, invite the children to put on their "x-ray eyes" (form circles around their eyes with their thumbs and forefingers) to visualize the whole word and spell all the letters in sequence, until the entire word has been erased. Repeat the game, with students selecting and erasing letters in the word.

- *Meet, Greet, and Read*: Write the set of word wall words on individual name tags and give one to each student. Provide some time for children to go around and "greet" as many of their classmates as possible, using the word on their name tag instead of their actual name.

- *Read It, Make It, Write It*: Students read each word in the first column, build it with magnetic letters, then write it on the white board. An alternative is to use a stamp pad to stamp the letters on paper.

Word Play All Day

Understanding that words are made up of sounds (phonological awareness) and that written letters correspond to spoken sounds (phonics) are critical concepts for beginning readers. However, if phonics instruction is to be truly effective in developing independent readers, it must be embedded in a total reading/language arts program (IRA, 1997).

Reading "Manipulatives" from the Dollar Store

- Magnifying glasses for word detectives
- Fancy sunglasses with the lenses removed to make "reading" glasses
- Magic wands and other pointers for tracking
- Fly swatters with a hole cut in the middle for word framing
- Plastic letters and containers to hold them
- Hand clappers to "put your hand on a word"

Concepts about print and features of language should be constantly reinforced all day long, in every component of the balanced literacy program. You'll find many ideas for teaching concepts about print and the phonetic principle in the chapters on reading and writing (Chapters 4, 5, and 6).

When children listen to stories read aloud, they expand their vocabularies, background experiences, and repertoire of language structures. Alphabet books are great tools for reinforcing letter names and initial consonant sounds, as children learn to connect familiar objects and pictures to alphabet letters and sounds. Even in ABC books, look for strong illustrations, text that flows naturally, and concepts that expand children's knowledge of their world.

Language concepts are an integral aspect of the shared reading experience. We always read the poem, chart, or story several times for meaning first, before isolating phrases, words, and letters. Once students are familiar with the story line or the concept load, we invite them to focus on print features. We use pointers to track words one at a time as we read. Any object with a hole in it can be used as a "framer" to isolate words. Students can use highlighting tape, sticky string, or highlighters to hunt for beginning and ending sounds, letter patterns, rhyming words, "words we know," and even punctuation.

During modeled writing, show students how to put spaghetti spaces between the letters and meatball spaces between the words.

Modeled writing provides an excellent opportunity to point out letter–sound relationships, phonetic patterns, and unique spellings of words. As we model the transfer of spoken language into print, we are showing students how to listen for sounds and to represent those sounds on paper. For example, we might demonstrate putting "spaghetti spaces" between the letters and "meatball spaces" between the words or "borrowing" a pattern from the word wall. Depending on the children's stage of readiness, we adjust our expectations for them to apply these strategies.

During shared and interactive writing activities, children learn that what they write matches what they say. Invented spelling is one of the most important tools for reinforcing both phonics and phonemic awareness by inviting children to experiment with what they know about letters and sounds and patterns. In this book, we refer to "bubble gum writing," (Chapter 6) which teaches students to pretend to stretch words out of their mouths like a piece of gum, writing a letter for every sound they hear.

Rhyming text not only has great appeal for young children, it also helps draw their attention to the rhythms of language, an important precursor to fluency. The beginning reading books by Dr. Seuss have been supporting children's literacy for decades, with ridiculous rhymes and rollicking rhythms that charm readers of all ages. We need to be careful with rhyming text, however. For every book with musical, natural text, there is one with contrived syntax ("*My breakfast I ate*") or rhymes that don't rhyme (*crack* and *trap*). Look for strong rhythm, rich language, interesting concepts and text features, and rhymes that actually rhyme.

Language play should be just that—play. It should be fast-paced and fun, with the goal of developing both knowledge and motivation to take an interest in how language goes together. As well, it should be differentiated and targeted to what students specifically need. When we integrate language play into all aspects of literacy learning, we demonstrate to children that language is both meaningful and authentic, while building both the skill and the will that are essential to literacy.

8

Celebrating Diversity in the Classroom

When Lori walked into the Kindergarten classroom of her neighborhood school not long ago, she was welcomed by Yazamin, who greeted Lori in English and her native Farsi. Yazamin and her mother and sister are newcomers from Iran; they haven't seen Yazamin's father for over a year and don't even know if he is alive. Alejandro doesn't have a mother, but he does have two fathers; he was adopted as a baby from an orphanage in Guatemala. Blonde-haired, blue-eyed Anika is here from Sweden for two years while her father is a visiting professor at a local university. When Benny first came to the class from China in the fall, his teachers couldn't get him to say a word; now they can't get him to stop talking.

Today's Kindergartens have a more diverse range of students than ever before. Some have had rich exposures to print and background experiences that make them ripe for learning to read. Others arrive at school with few literacy experiences in their own language or any other. Some speak only a language other than English, some are quite fluently multilingual, and some struggle with both the language of their home and their school. Often these are children whose culture is different from the dominant culture of their schools. In Toronto, Canada's largest city, 80 percent of children in public elementary schools have at least one parent born outside of Canada. Over half speak a first language other than English (O'Reilly & Yau, 2009). These children bring a range of cultural experiences, family traditions, and ways of knowing that make our school communities much richer but also more challenging.

Some researchers predict that by the year 2025, 49 percent of the students in U.S. schools will be children of color (Smolkin, 2003), yet the majority of teachers are white and middle class. Because the cultural makeup of the teaching profession has not caught up with the diversity of the students, there is often a disconnect between what multicultural learners bring to the classroom and what their teachers know and understand.

The National Association for the Education of Young Children (NAEYC) reports that, in the United States, demographic trends predict "dramatic increases in children's cultural and linguistic diversity and, unless conditions change, a greater share of children living in poverty" (NAEYC, 2009, 2). According to the Annie E. Casey Foundation's National KIDS COUNT Program, over 20 percent of American children live below the poverty line. We know that these children have fewer language and literacy experiences before school and are at greater risk of learning difficulties. We must reach and teach them all.

Our Most Vulnerable Learners

Kathryn Au (1993) has identified three factors that have an impact on children from diverse backgrounds: 1) the national or ethnic origin of one's ancestors; 2) socio-economic status; and 3) the language or dialect spoken in the home. Note that Au did not suggest that these children learn differently from other children, only that their *ways of knowing* are different. In our schools, we have tended to associate oral language facility and richness of experience with intelligence. As a result, the child who is verbal and articulate, who has had many experiences with print, and whose self-confidence has been nurtured by a safe and secure home life is frequently identified as gifted. On the other hand, we may overlook the gifts of the child who did not have the benefit of intellectual and verbal stimulation before school, or who may speak a first language other than English. We may label these students as "weak" when their only weakness has been a lack of experience with English words and print. It hardly needs to be said that it is unfair and inappropriate to correlate this lack of experience with lack of intelligence.

Different Ways of Knowing

All children come to school imbued in the habits of their families, sometimes in the traditions of a particular culture, and often in the rituals of a particular religion. We know that developmental milestones are the same, regardless of a child's background. However, cultural diversity has certain implications for literacy instruction, affecting the way children interact with print and what they know about story. As Shirley Brice Heath (1983) showed us long ago, children from middle-class homes in general succeed more easily in school because their ways of knowing and their literacy practices tend to match those of the school. However, all children come to school with "cultural capital," that is, a set of values and experiences based on their family lives. We must recognize and honor these ways of knowing as we plan instruction to meet the needs of all students. On the other hand, we cannot assume that all children from the same ethnic group will be the same in what they know, how they learn, and what they need.

Robert Slocumb and Ruby Payne's (2000) research on "cultures of poverty" tells us that language patterns vary, not just by nationality but also by socio-economic level. Even children whose first language is English may use nonstandard dialects that interfere with their ability to apply conventional letter–sound correspondences. Susan Neuman and Donna Celano (2001) also found that children in impoverished neighborhoods had less access to print, not just in their homes but also in their neighborhoods. Public signs were scarcer than in middle-class communities, contained less print, and were frequently obliterated by graffiti. Children from middle-class backgrounds are accustomed to hearing the formal language structures of school used in their homes. In lower socio-economic homes, speech tends to be of casual register. For example, according to Slocum and Payne, children in a professional family might be asked, "Would you please pick up the fork you dropped?" whereas children of poverty might hear, "Pick that up." That's why, in Betty Hart and Todd Risley's classic 1995 study, there was a 30-million-word gap between the number of words children from professional homes have heard before Kindergarten and the number of words children of poverty have heard. Within the culture of poverty, language is often sparse, informal, and functional. Because they are unfamiliar with formal registers of oral language, these children have more difficulty with written language as well as spoken directions. And because they don't understand, they may get frustrated and act out. Similarly, we teachers might get frustrated because students just "don't get it," despite repeated instructions.

In the same way, children of diverse cultures may have different models for using written language. Yazamin's mother reads story books to her in Farsi, reading from right to left and bottom to top. Benny's parents and grandparents use their limited English for filling out forms, writing checks, and performing other functional tasks, but they read only Mandarin newspapers. Dakota has never seen her grandmother pick up a book or a newspaper, but Dakota enjoys listening to the traditional tales and stories of when she was a young girl. Hearing oral storytelling in their first languages is an important experience for all children and a key step in their developing literacy. Even the words "once upon a time" do not mean the same thing to everyone. One of the ways we may penalize children of non-dominant cultures is in our heavy use of the time-linear story as a literacy tool. For example, some Asian cultures start with the middle of the story, then move to the beginning, and then to the end. In the oral tradition of many African-American homes, storytelling often begins at the part that has the most emotional appeal to the listeners and often ends with the storyteller's observations about the characters and their motives (Slocumb & Payne, 2000). We must remember that our sense of story is just a cultural convention.

Honoring Families

Perhaps the best way to show respect for our students' cultural backgrounds is by taking the time to learn about where they come from, how they live, and how they see the world. This understanding must always involve reaching out on our part, because the parents we most need to meet are often those who are least likely to come walking into our classrooms. Many parents are intimidated about attending school events. Self-consciousness over language proficiency, negative memories of their own school experiences, and worry about what they might hear about their children all contribute to their discomfort. It is important to involve parents first in events that are social and nonthreatening. When schools invite the community to turkey suppers or pancake breakfasts, the parents are likely to feel more comfortable attending academic events, such as assemblies and parent–teacher conferences. Parents who feel welcome in the school are more supportive of its programs and more inclined to collaborate with teachers in their children's education. There are many ways in which schools have endeavored to make all parents feel part of the school community:

- inviting parents into classrooms to share their knowledge and expertise, whether of culture, tradition, work, or talents.
- organizing festive events that welcome the entire neighborhood, not just the school community, with food and celebration.
- offering childcare for preschoolers so parents can attend parent–teacher conferences and other school events.
- making home visits and sending notes to children at home.
- communicating with praise and compliments as well as concerns and problems with the students.
- adjusting expectations for home reading and other homework support.

- hiring (or finding volunteer) community workers whose role it is to liaise with cultural groups in their own languages to explain school programs, translate printed materials, and raise parents' concerns with the school.
- creating parenting centres where parents can bring preschoolers to play, network with other parents, and learn to speak English.
- making translators available for school assemblies and other events and printing portions of the school newsletter in languages other than English.
- establishing predictable routines, such as sending home all printed information in a "Friday package," so parents know when to expect communication and can have it all translated at once, if necessary.

What Children Need

How do we help our most vulnerable learners? By believing in their competency and capability. By listening and helping to give them a voice. As educators, we need to provide the tools, the language, and the time to support all learners. More importantly, we need to build relationships.

Taking the time to build strong relationships with the children and their families allows educators to identify personal learning styles. Once we know how they approach learning (in their different ways), we can better support them.

By listening and believing in children's ideas, watching and observing their actions and interactions through play, we can gauge some of their intentions, allowing us to challenge and extend their learning and create authentic, meaningful experiences.

Lisa Commisso. Early Childhood Educator

We know that children who are culturally, linguistically, and socio-economically diverse are at greater risk of struggling in school, especially with literacy. We also know that these vulnerable children are over-represented in special education (Obiakor, 2006). Although opportunities for play, inquiry, discovery, and social interaction are essential to a well-rounded Kindergarten experience, they are not enough for all learners. Fortunately, we also know more now about best practices in literacy instruction for our most vulnerable learners. There used to be a common misconception that children with limited experience with print simply need more "skill and drill." In her award-winning doctoral dissertation, Nell Duke (2000) found that first grade children in schools in poor neighborhoods were offered quite different print environments than their peers in affluent districts. These children had fewer opportunities to interact with print, to engage in writing, and to read connected text; instead they spent more time engaged in activities such as copying, taking dictation, and completing worksheets. As a result, the literacy disadvantage with which these children began was exacerbated by a lack of opportunities for engaging with connected text. Meanwhile, their more advantaged peers spent time engaged in authentic reading experiences, perpetuating what Stanovich called "the Matthew effect" (1994, 281); in other words, the rich got richer and the poor got poorer.

Patricia Cunningham and Richard Allington assert that children of poverty, even more than other students, need a "print-rich, story-rich, book-rich" classroom experience (1997, 209). These are the children who depend on school to become literate. They need daily opportunities and large blocks of time to read and write (Au, 2000; Strickland, 2008). They need exposure to many types and genres of books to develop the vocabulary and experiential base that was lacking in their preschool experiences. They need to be engaged in meaningful and motivational literacy activities that help them develop positive attitudes toward reading. Of course, they also need purposeful and explicit instruction in phonological awareness, the phonetic principle, and comprehension strategies, all applied in the context of real reading and writing. They still need intensive practice to build automaticity in decoding and reading high-frequency words. Most of all, they need teachers who constantly monitor their progress and adjust instruction accordingly. As Janet Mort suggests in her comprehensive treatise on vulnerable learners, "As educators we must use assessment, teaching and tracking progress–just like scientists to ensure that we are doing the right thing. There is no room for guesswork when it comes to children's lives" (2014).

In other words, our vulnerable learners need the same good instruction that all children should receive. Catherine Snow and her colleagues asserted, in the classic study they labeled "Unfulfilled Expectations," "There is little evidence that children experiencing difficulties learning to read, even those with identifiable learning disabilities, need radically different sorts of supports than children at low risk, although they may need much more intensive support. Excellent instruction is the best intervention for children who demonstrate problems learning to read" (1998, 32).

Good Kindergarten classroom instruction will be enough to guide most students on their first steps to literacy. For those students who do not experience success, special interventions and adaptations may be necessary. These interventions should be a) targeted, intensive and short-term; b) take place with individuals and in small groups, rather than in whole-class instruction; and c) supplement the classroom program, rather than replace it (Cunningham and Allington, 2007). A comprehensive, early childhood longitudinal study (ELS-K) reported major academic gains for children who received 30 to 60 percent of additional instructional time in reading and math within a child-centred, play-oriented Kindergarten program (Snyder et al., 2014).

In the past few years, we have observed our youngest learners bringing a vastly different skill set to school. They are much more comfortable with a touchscreen phone or tablet than they are holding a pencil, crayon, scissors, book, or another traditional learning tool. Our teachers are prepared for many of our students to enter their classrooms knowing little about letters, numbers, sharing, or colors, as often, Kindergarten is their very first exposure to both head and heart learning in a calm and structured setting. These teachers look at each unique learner and find a special spark from which to build success. They model and develop a passion for learning and an understanding of the importance of working together.

In Kindergarten, not only are our teachers growing readers, mathematicians, and scientists who possess an academic-growth mindset, they are relentless in developing scholars equipped with the vocabulary and skills needed both academically and socially for college, career, and citizenship. What an awesome privilege and responsibility to work each day with children who will one day grow up to make their community and our world a better place!

Christine Thomas, K-2 Instructional Leader

Setting challenging but achievable learning goals for our students, and consistently monitoring their progress towards those goals, enables us to plan instruction that takes every student to higher levels of literacy. Good teachers know that there is no single method or approach that will be effective for all students. They have a repertoire of strategies for assessing student progress, implementing a balanced program of instruction, and providing interventions, as necessary, to take all students to higher levels of development. Ultimately, it is the teacher who makes the difference for students. Janet Mort equates literacy instruction with stepping stones across a pond, suggesting that teachers "offer multiple routes to the other side of the pond–giving children choices that support their comfort levels; offering them challenges, providing alternatives, creating safe places where they can linger and practice; designing a privacy screen that allows them dignity; and making sure that their individual path is just right for them" (2014, v).

Occasionally, we are fortunate enough to run into students we taught years ago. They are teachers and dentists, athletes and musicians, moms and dads. We are honored to think that we had a role in their journey from the Kindergarten scientists and early readers of yesterday to the literate citizens of today. Twenty years from now, when today's standards and initiatives are dim memories, our students will be full-grown testimony to the art and skill we brought to our classrooms when they were young. We know that every year in school is important, but surely no single year is more vital than Kindergarten. The routines we establish, the skills, strategies, and concepts we teach, and the expectations we hold will influence our students for the rest of their lives. That's a significant obligation and responsibility; it's also an exciting opportunity. Let's make the most of it.

Resources

Adams, M.J. (1990) *Beginning to Read: Thinking and Learning About Print.* Cambridge, MA: MIT Press.

Anderson, R.C., Hiebert, E.H., Scott, J.A., & Wilkinson, I.A.G. (1985) "Becoming a Nation of Readers: The Report of the Commission on Reading." Washington, DC: National Institute of Education.

Au, K.H. (2000) "Literacy instruction for young children of diverse backgrounds" in D.S. Strickland & L.M. Morrow (eds.), *Beginning Reading and Writing.* New York: Teachers College Press; Newark, DE: International Reading Association, 35-46.

Ball, D. J. (2002) *Playgrounds: Risks, Benefits and Choices.* London: Health and Safety Executive.

Barbour, A.C. (1996) "Physical Competence and Peer Relations in 2nd Graders: Qualitative Case Studies from Recess Play." *Journal of Research in Childhood Education*, 11, 35-46.

Beck, I., McKeown, M., & Kucan, L. (2002) *Bringing Words to Life: Robust Vocabulary Instruction.* New York: Guilford.

Betts, E. (1946) *Foundations of Reading Instruction: With Emphasis on Differentiated Guidance.* New York: American Book.

Biemiller, A. (2003) "Teaching Vocabulary in the Primary Grades: Vocabulary Instruction Needed" in J. Bauman and E. Kame'euni (eds.), *Vocabulary Instruction: Research to Practice.* New York: Guilford.

Bissett, D. (1969) "The Amount and Effect of Recreational Reading in Selected Fifth Grade Classes," Unpublished doctoral dissertation, Syracuse University.

Bjorklund, D.F. & Gardiner, A.K. (2011) "Object Play and Tool Use: Developmental and Evolutionary Perspectives" in A.D. Pellegrini (ed.), *Oxford Handbook of Play.* Oxford, UK: Oxford University Press, 153-171.

Boushey, G., & Moser, J. (2006) *The Daily Five: Fostering Literacy Independence in the Elementary Grades.* Portland, ME: Stenhouse.

Brice Heath, S. (1983). *Ways with Words: Language, Life and Work in Communities and Classrooms.* Cambridge, UK: Cambridge University Press.

Britton, J. (1970) *Language and Learning.* Coral Gables, FL: University of Miami Press.

Brookfield, J., Norris, M., Baldo, M., Brown, M., & Brummell, L. (2013) "Embedding Effective Instruction in Games to Teach Code-Related Early Literacy Skills." Paper presented at the 58th Annual Conference of the International Literacy Association, San Antonio TX.

Calhoun, E. (1999) *Teaching Beginning Reading and Writing with the Picture Word Inductive Model.* Alexandria, VA: Association for Supervision and Curriculum Development.

Canadian Language and Literacy Research Network (2009) *National Strategy for Early Literacy*. London, ON: University of Western Ontario. http://eyeonkids.ca/docs/files/national_strategy_for_early_literacy_report%5B1%5D.pdf

Clay, M. (1967) "The Reading Behaviour of Five-Year-Old Children: A Research Report." *New Zealand Journal of Educational Studies*, 2, 11-31.

Clay, M.M. (1991) *Becoming Literate: The Construction of Inner Control*. Portsmouth, NH: Heinemann.

Collins, K. (2008) "Supporting Children's Book Choice" in K. Szymusiak, F. Sibberson, & L. Koch (eds.), *Beyond Leveled Books: Early and Transitional Readers in Grades K-5*, 2nd ed. Portland, ME: Stenhouse, 72-74.

Cronin, D. (2003) *Diary of a Worm*. New York: Harper-Collins.

Cunningham, P., & Allington, R. (2007) *Classrooms that Work: They Can All Read and Write*. New York: Addison-Wesley.

Dickinson, D.K. (1989) "Effects of a Shared Reading Program on One Head Start Language and Literacy Environment," in J.B. Allen & J.M. Mason (eds.), *Risk Makers, Risk Takers, Risk Breakers: Reducing the Risks*. Portsmouth, NH: Heinemann, 125-153.

———. (2001) "Large-Group and Free-Play Times: Conversational Settings Supporting Language and Literacy Development" in D.K. Dickinson & P.O. Tabors (eds.), *Beginning Literacy with Language: Young Children Learning at Home and School*. Baltimore, MD: Brookes Publishing, 223-55.

Doake, D. (1988) *Reading Begins at Birth*. New York: Scholastic.

Duke, N. (2004) "The Case for Informational Text," in *Educational Leadership* 61:6, ASCD, 40-44. http://www.ascd.org/publications/educational-leadership/mar04/vol61/num06/The-Case-for-Informational-Text.aspx

Duke, N.K. (2000a) "3-6 Minutes per Day: The Scarcity of Informational Texts in First Grade." *Reading Research Quarterly*, 35:2, 202-224. doi:10.1598/RRQ.35.2.1

Durkin. D. (1966) "The Achievement of Pre-school Readers: Two Longitudinal Studies," in *Reading Research Quarterly*. 1, 5-36.

Emig, J. (1977) "Writing as a Mode of Learning." *College Composition and Communication*, 28:2, May, NCTE, 122-128.

Fielding, L., Wilson, P., & Anderson, R. (1986) "A New Focus on Free Reading: The Role of Trade Books in Reading Instruction" in T. Raphael (ed.), *The Contexts of School-Based Literacy*. New York: Random House, 149-60.

Fisher, A.V., Godwin, K., & Seltman, H. (2014) "Visual Environment, Attention Allocation, and Learning in Young Children: When Too Much of a Good Thing May Be Bad." *Psychological Science*, 25:7, 1362-70.

Fjørtoft, I. (2001) "The Natural Environment as a Playground for Children: The Impact of Outdoor Play Activities in Pre-Primary School Children." *Early Childhood Education Journal*, 29:2.

Gambrell, L.B. & Dromsky, A. (2000) "Fostering Reading Comprehension" in D.S. Strickland & L.M. Morrow (eds.), *Beginning Reading and Writing*. New York: Teachers College Press; Newark, DE: International Reading Association, 143-54.

Gonoski, T. (2015) *Creating a Yes Environment*. Community Playthings. www.communityplaythings.com/resources/articles/2015/creating-a-yes-environment

Government of British Columbia. (2010) *Full Day Kindergarten Program Guide*.

Government of Ontario. (2016) *The Kindergarten Program*.

Government of Ontario. (2016) *21st Century Competencies: Foundation Document for Discussion.*

Graham, S. & Hebert, M. (2010) *Writing to Read: Evidence for How Writing Can Improve Reading.* New York: Carnegie Corporation.

Graves, D. (1983) *Writing: Teachers and Children at Work.* Portsmouth, NH: Heinemann.

Graves, M. (ed.) (2009) *Essential Readings on Vocabulary Instruction.* Newark, DE: International Reading Association.

Gray, P. (2014) "Why Children Love It and Need It." Psychologytoday.com, April 7, 2014. https://www.psychologytoday.com/blog/freedom-learn/201404/risky-play-why-children-love-it-and-need-it

Hanline, M.F., Milton, S., & Phelps, P.C. (2010) "The Relationship Between Preschool Block Play and Reading and Maths Abilities in Early Elementary School: A Longitudinal Study of Children with and without Disabilities," in *Early Child Development and Care*, 180:8, 1005–17.

Harste, J., Woodward, V., & Burke, C. (1984) *Language Stories and Literacy Lessons.* Portsmouth, NH: Heinemann.

Hart, B. & Risley, T. (1995) *Meaningful Differences in the Everyday Experience of Young Americn Children.* Baltimore, MD: Paul H. Brookes.

Hayes, D. P. & Ahrens, M. (1988). "Vocabulary Simplification for Children: A Special Case of 'Motherese'," in *Journal of Child Language*, 15, 395–410.

Henkes, K. (2008) *Chrysanthemum.* New York: Harper-Collins.

Hiebert, E.H. & Raphael, T.E. (1998) *Early Literacy Instruction.* Fort Worth, TX: Harcourt Brace.

Holdaway, D. (1979) *The Foundations of Literacy.* Sydney, Australia: Ashton Scholastic.

International Reading Association & National Association for the Education of Young Children. (1998) "Learning to Read and Write: Developmentally Appropriate Practices for Children." *The Reading Teacher*, 52:2, 193–216.

International Reading Association. (1998) "Phonemic Awareness and the Teaching of Reading: A Position Statement from the Board of Directors of the International Reading Association." Newark, DE.

Jones, C.D., Reutzel, D.R., & Fargo, J.D. (2010). "Comparing Two Methods of Writing Instruction: Effects on Kindergarten Students' Reading Skills." *The Journal of Educational Research* 103:5, 327-341.

Jones, Cindy D., Clark, Sarah K., & Reutzel, D. Ray. (2012) "Enhancing Alphabet Knowledge Instruction: Research Implications and Practical Strategies for Early Childhood Educators." TEaL Faculty Publications. Paper 404. http://digitalcommons.usu.edu/teal_facpub/404

Justice, L.M., Pence, K., Bowles, R.B., & Wiggins, A. (2006) "An Investigation of Four Hypotheses Concerning the Order by Which 4-year-old Children Learn the Alphabet Letters." *Early Childhood Research Quarterly*, 21, 374-389.

Kagan, S. & Lowenstein, A. (2004) "School Readiness and Children's Play: Contemporary Oxymoron or Compatible Option?" in E. Zigler, D. Singer, & S. Bishop-Josef (eds.), *Children's Play: The Roots of Reading.* Washington, DC: Zero to Three Press, 59–76.

Krasnor, L.R. & Pepler, D.J. (1980) "The Study of Children's Play: Some Suggested Future Directions." *New Directions for Child and Adolescent Development*, 1980, 85–95. doi:10.1002/cd.23219800908

LaBerge, D. & Samuels, S. J. (1974) "Toward a Theory of Automatic Information Processing in Reading." *Cognitive Psychology*, 6, 293-323.

Langer, J. (1996) *Envisioning Literature: Literary Understanding and Literature Instruction*. New York: Teachers College Press.

Marcon, R. (2002) "Moving Up the Grades: Relationship Between Preschool Model and Later School Success." *Early Childhood Research & Practice*, 4:1.

Martin, B. (2010) *Brown Bear, Brown Bear, What Do You See?* New York: Henry Holt.

Martinez, M. & Roser, N. (1985) "Read It Again: The Value of Repeated Readings During Storytime." *The Reading Teacher*, 38:8, 782-86.

Martinez, M. & Teale, W. (1988) "Reading in a Kindergarten Classroom Library." *The Reading Teacher*, 41:6, 568-72.

McGee, L.M. & Richgels, D.J. (2003) *Designing Early Literacy Programs: Strategies for At-Risk Preschool and Kindergarten Children*. New York: Guilford.

McGee, L.M. & Schickedanz, J.A. (2007) "Repeated Interactive Read-alouds in Preschool and Kindergarten." *The Reading Teacher*, 60:8, 742-51. doi:10.1598/RT.60.8.4

McGill-Franzen, A. (2006) *Kindergarten Literacy: Matching Assessment and Instruction in Kindergarten*. New York: Scholastic.

Morphett, M. & Washburne, C. (1931) "When Should Children Begin to Read?" *The Elementary School Journal*, 31:7, 496-503.

Morrow, L.M. & Asbury, E. (2003) "Current Practices in Early Literacy Development" in L.M. Morrow, L.B. Gambrell, & M. Pressley (eds.), *Best Practices in Literacy Instruction*, 2nd ed. New York: Guilford, 43–63.

Morrow, L.M., O'Connor, E.M., & Smith, J.K. (1990) "Effects of a Story Reading Program on the Literacy Development of At-Risk Kindergarten Children." *Journal of Reading Behavior*, 22:3, 255-75.

Mort, J. (2014) *Joyful Literacy Interventions: Early Learning Classroom Essentials*.

Most, B. (1996) *Cock-a-Doodle-Moo!* New York: Houghton Mifflin Harcourt.

Munsch, R. (1980) *The Paper Bag Princess*. Toronto: Annick Press.

National Association for the Education of Young Children. (2009) "Developmentally Appropriate Practice in Early Childhood Programs Serving Children from Birth Through Age 8" (Position statement). Washington, DC. Retrieved May 5, 2011, from www.naeyc.org/files/naeyc/file/positions/position%20statement%20Web.pdf

National Center for Education Statistics. (2000) "Early Childhood Longitudinal Study of Kindergarten." ECLS-K.

National Early Literacy Panel. (2008) "Developing Early Literacy: Report of the National Early Literacy Panel."

National Reading Panel (U.S.) & National Institute of Child Health and Human Development (U.S.). (2000) "Report of the National Reading Panel: Teaching Children to Read: An Evidence-based Assessment of the Scientific Research Literature on Reading and Its Implications for Reading Instruction: Reports of the Subgroups." Washington, DC: National Institute of Child Health and Human Development, National Institutes of Health.

Neuman, S.B. & Celano, D. (2001) "Access to Print in Low-income and Middle-income Communities: An Ecological Study of Four Neighborhoods." *Reading Research Quarterly*, 36:1, 8-26. doi:10.1598/RRQ.36.1.1

Newman, S.B., Newman, E.H., & Dwyer, J. (2011) "Educational Effects of a Vocabulary Intervention on Preschoolers' Word Knowledge and Conceptual Development: A Cluster-Randomized Trial." *Reading Research Quarterly* 46:3, September 2011, 249-272.

O'Reilly, J. & Yau, M. (2009) "2008 Parent Census, Kindergarten–Grade 6: System Overview and Detailed Findings." Toronto: Toronto District School Board.

Obiakor, F. (2006) *Multicultural Special Education: Culturally Responsive Teaching*. Upper Saddle River, NJ: Merrill.

Ouvry, M. (2003) *Exercising Muscles and Minds–Outdoor Play and the Early Years Curriculum*. London: National Children's Bureau.

Packet, M.B. & Diffily, D. (2004) *Teaching Young Children: An Introduction to the Early Childhood Profession*. Clifton Park, NY: Delmar Cengage.

Paley, V. (2004) *A Child's Work: The Importance of Fantasy Play*. Chicago: University of Chicago Press.

Parkes, Brenda. (2000) *Read it Again! Revisiting Shared Reading*. Portland, ME: Stenhouse.

Pellegrini, A.D. & Davis, P. (1993) "Relations Between Children's Playground and Classroom Behaviors." *American Educational Research Journal*, 32, 845-864.

Play Safety Forum. (2002) "Managing Risk in Play Provision: A Position Statement." London: Children's Play Council.

Reeves, D.B. (2000) "The 90/90/90 Schools: A Case Study" in *Accountability in Action: A Blueprint for Learning Organizations*, 2nd ed. Denver, CO: Advanced Learning Press, 185-208.

Rog, L.J. (2013) *Guiding Readers: Making the Most of the 18-minute Guided Reading Lesson*. Markham, ON: Pembroke.

———. (2015) *Marvelous Minilessons for Teaching Nonfiction Writing K–3*. Markham, ON: Pembroke.

Rubin, K.H., Fein, G., & Vandenberg, B. (1983) "Play" in E.M. Hetherington (ed.), *Handbook of Child Psychology: Socialization, Personality, and Social Development*, 4. New York: Wiley.

Russ, S. & Wallace, C. (2014) "Pretend Play and Creative Process." *American Journal of Play* 6:1, 136-147.

Russell, J.L. (2011) "From Child's Garden to Academic Press: The Role of Shifting Institutional Logics in Redefining Kindergarten Education." *American Educational Research Journal*, 48:2, 236–267.

Scanlon, D., Anderson, K., & Sweeney, J. (2011) *Early Intervention for Reading Difficulties: The Interactive Strategies Approach*. New York: Guilford.

Schickedanz, J. (2004) "A Framework and Suggested Guidelines for Pre-Kindergarten Content Standards." *The Reading Teacher*, 2004, 58:1, 95-97.

Shephard, R.J. (1983) "Physical Activity and the Healthy Mind." *Canadian Medical Association Journal*, 128, 525-530.

Slocumb, P.D. & Payne, R.K. (2000) *Removing the Mask: Giftedness in Poverty*. Highlands, TX: RFT.

Smolkin, L.B. & Donovan, C.A. (2003) "Supporting Comprehension Acquisition for Emerging and Struggling Readers: The Interactive Information Book Read Aloud." *Exceptionality*, 11, 25-38.

Snell, C.A. (2007) "The Impact of Daily Writing on Kindergarten Students' Phonemic Awareness." Walden University. gradworks.umi.com/32/61/3261224.html

Snow, C.E., Burns, M.S., & Griffin, P. (1998) *Preventing Reading Difficulties in Young Children*. Washington, DC: National Academy Press.

Snyder, T.D., de Brey, C., & Dillow, S.A. (2016) *Digest of Education Statistics 2014*. Washington, DC: National Center for Education Statistics, Institute of Education Sciences, U.S. Department of Education.

Southall, M. (2009) *Differentiated Small-Group Reading Lessons*. New York: Scholastic.

Stahl, R.J. (1994) "Using Think-Time and Wait-Time Skillfully in the Classroom." *ERIC Digest*. http://www.ericdigests.org/1995-1/think.htm

Stanovich, K. (1994) "Romance and Reality." *The Reading Teacher*, 47:4, 280–291.

Stead, T. (2006) *Reality Checks: Teaching Reading Comprehension with Nonfiction K-5*. Portland, ME: Stenhouse.

Stead, T. (2011) *Should There Be Zoos? A Persuasive Text*. New York: Mondo Press.

Stipek, D., Feiler, R., Daniels, D., & Milburn, S. (1995) "Effects of Different Instructional Approaches on Young Children's Achievement and Motivation." *Child Development*, 66:1, 209-23.

Strickland, D. (2008) "When DAP Meets GAP: Promoting Peaceful Coexistence Between Developmentally Appropriate Practice." www.docstoc.com/docs/37059391/When-DAP-Meets-GAP-Promoting-Peaceful-Coexistence-Between-

Sulzby, E. (1985) "Children's Emergent Reading of Favorite Storybooks: A Developmental Study. *Reading Research Quarterly*, 20:4, 458-81. doi:10.1598/RRQ.20.4.4

Teale, W. H. & McKay, R. (2015) *No More Teaching a Letter a Week*. Portsmouth, NH: Heinemann.

Tolhurst, M. (1994) *Somebody and the Three Blairs*. New York: Scholastic.

Van Horn, M.L., Karlin, E.O., Ramey, S.L., Aldridge, J., & Snyder, S.W. (2005) "Effects of Developmentally Appropriate Practices on Children's Development: A Review of Research and Discussion of Methodological and Analytic Issues." *Elementary School Journal* 105:4, 325-51.

Vygotsky, L.S. (1978) *Mind in Society: The Development of Higher Psychological Processes* (M. Cole, V. John-Steiner, S. Scribner, & E. Souberman, eds. & trans.). Cambridge, MA: Harvard University Press.

Ward, C. (1997) *Cookie's Week*. New York: Puffin Books.

Weisberg, D. S., Hirsh-Pasek, K., & Golinkoff, R.M. (2013) "Guided Play: Where Curriculum Goals Meet a Playful Pedagogy." *Journal Compilation*, 7:2, International Mind, Brain, and Education Society and Blackwell.

Welsch, J. (2008) "Playing Within and Beyond the Story: Encouraging Book-Related Pretend Play." *The Reading Teacher*, 62:2, 138-48.

White, R.E. (2012) *The Power of Play: A Research Summary on Play and Learning*. Minneapolis, MN: Minnesota Children's Museum.

Index